Introduction

The earlier Kittiwake guide to the waterfalls of North & Mid Wales gave a brief introduction to the many waterfalls to be found in this area. This book deals with a few of the many remaining more obvious ones, plus some that are a little more obscure. Nevertheless the walks described herein are all wonderful undertakings.

A few of these walks are very short whilst some waterfalls can even be seen from the comfort of your car or from a car park. But to hear a waterfall increase in noise as it is approached excites the mind and is part of the adventure.

It is better to visit waterfalls during, or immediately after, a period of rainfall, when they will all be at their best. But it is important to remember that approaching waterfalls from above, to get a better view, is NOT recommended due to slippery rocks and loose edges. These walks take you to the best *safe* vantage points. Bathing in plunge pools is also NOT recommended due to hidden dangers brought in during floods, such as sunken trees and wire fencing, which can easily trap the unwary.

It is very likely that these walks will be done in wet weather, so it is important to wear good walking boots, appropriate clothing and waterproofs. Tree roots become slippery, as do stones, when moisture seems to awaken lichen, making them lethal obstacles at times. Few of these walks venture very high into the mountains, but some do rise above the tree line. These more exposed walks become susceptible to much poorer weather including mist, wind and of course driving rain. On a much brighter note sunny days after a summer rainstorm can also provide a memorable sight, when brown water contrasts strongly with the greenery of the trees.

Some walks have picnic tables en route, and these are mentioned in the text. There is often a café or a pub nearby. The walks have detailed descriptions including how to reach the start, a brief resumé and a map. Map references for the start are given as an extra aid to location.

Much of the flora around waterfalls is quite rare, as well as being home for amphibious creatures. Please respect their habitat and leave plants and flowers for others to see.

All the walks described have been individually walked and checked but as with all guide books, access and conditions change. It would be very useful if you do find any errors to contact me via the publisher so that the walk can be checked and corrections made to the next edition. The walk into Cwm Idwal includes the highest single drop waterfall in Wales, but this occurs *only* after a spell of wet weather. This is the spectacular 305 feet high Devil's Appendix.

Enjoy your walking!

WALK 1
ABER FALLS, Rhaeadr Fawr & Rhaeadr Fach

DESCRIPTION This is a really great walk, initially through woodland, to one of Wales' most famous waterfalls before ascending and crossing open sheep grazing hillsides. There are superb views across to Puffin Island and Anglesey on this section. The easy approach to the main waterfall, Rhaeadr Fawr, is reached by an all ability trail. A slightly steeper section near the falls will need a little help for those without electric wheelchairs. The falls are a famous landmark. Allow 2½ hours walking time for the 4½ miles circular route. There are many opportunities for picnicking. The all-ability there and back walk is 2½ miles for which 2 hours should be allowed. There are toilets and an accessible toilet in the main car park.

START At the parking area close to Bont Newydd.

DIRECTIONS Travelling from the east or west along the A55 turn into the village of Abergwyngregyn. At the sign for the falls follow the narrow road up through the village to the parking area on the right very close to Bont Newydd. There is a larger car park (small fee) after crossing the bridge from where the all ability trail commences.

1 From the car parking area before Bont Newydd go through the kissing gate and past the information board. Follow the good path alongside the Afon Rhaeadr Fawr to reach a footbridge. Cross this and go through the gate to join a gravel track. (The all-ability trail, coming up from the left, is joined here). TURN RIGHT up this to enter Coedydd Aber. Pass to the right of a peculiar barrel shaped shelter and through the kissing gate. Continue following the track as it rises gently to the Visitor Centre at Nant. Keep on the track and through the next gate and another to where the track shrinks to a wide gravel path. Ignore steps to the left and continue past a footbridge seen to the right to reach the larger waterfall, Rhaeadr Fawr. *This is a very fine spectacle especially in flood or when frozen.* (If doing the all-ability walk, return to the car park by the same way).

2 Return a short distance and descend some steps to the footbridge on the left. Cross this and walk up a flight of steps to a level grassy area. Go through the gate on the right and follow the clear but rough path. Continue to another footbridge above which is the smaller waterfall, Rhaeadr Fach. At the far side of the bridge the path continues to reach a 'Y' junction and marker post. BEAR RIGHT on the wide grassy path. Cross a stream and continue uphill then along to another marker post at a 'Y' junction. GO RIGHT and continue past another marker post. BEAR RIGHT and through a gate. Continue up the path that quickly widens to a track. Go through the next gate. The track continues gradually up and passes below power lines immediately after passing through a gate.

3 The track continues to rise gradually to where it levels and begins to descend gradually. *Lovely views of Puffin Island, the coast and Anglesey develop.* Continue through a gate and continue through the next gate where there is a marker post indicating the North Wales Coastal Path to the left. GO RIGHT here down the track. At the low marker post TURN RIGHT as indicated. Follow the narrow path across the hillside to where it steepens considerably. Descend and go through a gate. A further steep descent leads to a fence. BEAR RIGHT to go through a gate and walk down to the narrow road. TURN RIGHT and walk up the road back to the car park.

*C*lose *to the falls an information board explains that the pile of stones to the side of the path are in fact the remains of a round house from circa 2,000 – 2,700 years ago. The standing stone in the pile of stones has been dated to approximately 2,000 BC.*

Aber, although small, is an interesting and a historically important little village. A large, grassy, circular mound is very prominent and is known as Llewelyn's Mound.

WALK 1

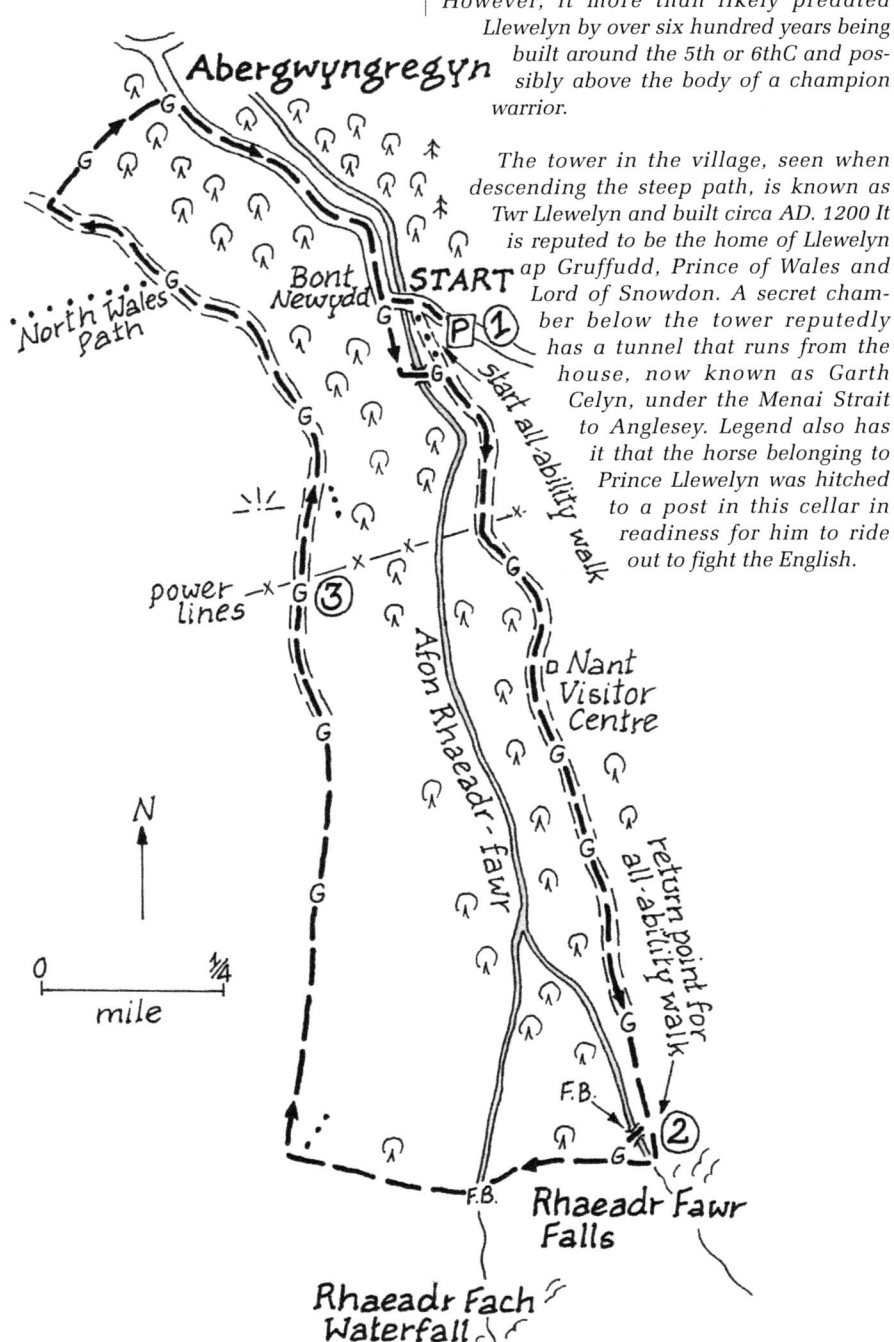

However, it more than likely predated Llewelyn by over six hundred years being built around the 5th or 6thC and possibly above the body of a champion warrior.

The tower in the village, seen when descending the steep path, is known as Twr Llewelyn and built circa AD. 1200 It is reputed to be the home of Llewelyn ap Gruffudd, Prince of Wales and Lord of Snowdon. A secret chamber below the tower reputedly has a tunnel that runs from the house, now known as Garth Celyn, under the Menai Strait to Anglesey. Legend also has it that the horse belonging to Prince Llewelyn was hitched to a post in this cellar in readiness for him to ride out to fight the English.

WALK 2
GREY MARE'S TAIL
Rhaeadr y Parc Mawr

DESCRIPTION This is a lovely and easy ¾ mile stroll to a very pretty waterfall taking 30 minutes. Set in some lovely woodland the way is easy to follow. The return walk is down a quiet road with a short section along a busier one.

START At the Snowdonia National Park parking area named Coed Felin Blwm.

DIRECTIONS Follow the B5106 from Betws y Coed towards Trefriw. TURN RIGHT at the 'T' junction close to Gwydir Castle and LEFT at the 'T' junction 10 yards ahead. Continue for 300 yards and TURN LEFT immediately beyond the first house, Melin Blwm. There is a partially hidden car park sign and the Snowdonia National Park sign for Coed Felin Blwm (Lead Mill Wood). Drive through the gate to the small car park 50 yards ahead.

Follow the obvious gravel path from the car park up to a level area. Cross the footbridge and continue to reach the fine falls. The path continues up some steps from where, near to the top of these, there is a lovely view of Trefriw and the Conwy Valley. At the top climb over a ladder stile to reach a narrow tarmac road. TURN LEFT and follow this crossing over the stream that forms the waterfall to another 'T' junction. TURN LEFT down the road to reach another 'T' junction. TURN LEFT then LEFT again at the next 'T' junction 10 yards ahead. Continue along this road and TURN LEFT just past Melin Blwm. Go through the gate to the car parking area.

Just before reaching the waterfall and on the left are the ruins of Felin Blwm lead mill. Established by the Gwydir Estate, lead ore from Parc Lead Mine, opened in 1855, was crushed and treated. During the decline in the demand for lead the mill became a saw-mill, finally closing in 1963. The water flowing down the waterfall comes from Parc Lead Mine.

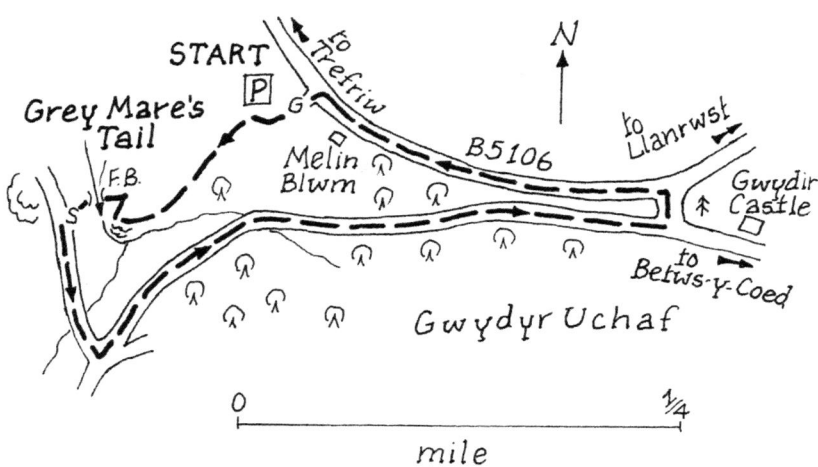

WALKS 2 & 3

WALK 3
FAIRY FALLS
Rhaeadr y Tylwyth Teg

DESCRIPTION A pleasant walk of ½ mile for which 25 minutes will suffice. Although situated in the lovely village of Trefriw the walk follows the Afon Crafnant to a very fine viewpoint for the falls.

START At the car park 100 yards down the road opposite the Woollen Mills.

DIRECTIONS Follow the B5106 from Betws y Coed towards Trefriw. TURN RIGHT at the 'T' junction close to Gwydir Castle and LEFT at the 'T' junction 10 yards ahead. Continue into the village of Trefriw. TURN RIGHT opposite the Woollen Mill to the unsigned car park on the right. This is really just a long lay-by. There are toilets on the left just after the turning.

Return to the B5106 and cross over. TURN RIGHT and continue over the footbridge. Opposite the Fairy Falls Hotel TURN LEFT and LEFT again 30 yards up the hill where there is a finger post. A way marker indicates number 4. The path passes above several small falls down to the left. At the footbridge on the left continue STRAIGHT on and not across the bridge. Another way marker numbered 4 directs. There is now a substantial green metal fence on the left. Continue to the falls where there is a rustic seat to admire these pretty falls. Follow the path from behind the seat up to way markers. Before following the direction indicated by way marker 4 go on to the bridge for a great view of the falls. From the way markers follow the wide path that bends left to join a road. TURN RIGHT and RIGHT again at the next junction to reach the B5106. TURN RIGHT and return to the car park.

Trefriw today is mostly known for its woollen mills. There is a nearby chalybeate spa, first known to have been used by the Romans. It was developed further around 1700. The spa was one of very few in Europe that classified chalybeate water as a medicine. This is due to the high iron content.

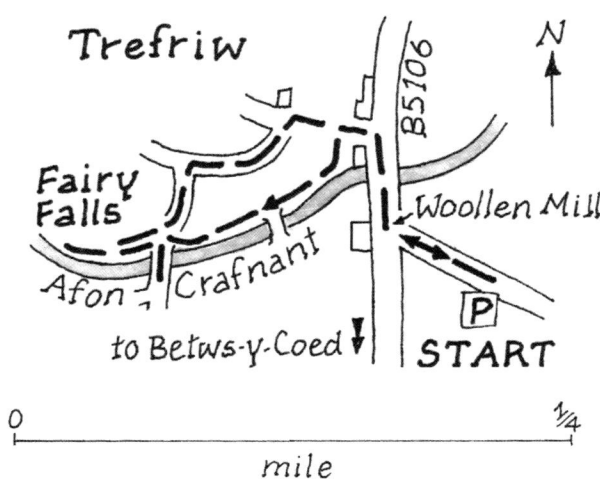

WALK 4
GARTH FALLS

DESCRIPTION This very pleasant and easy ¾ mile stroll takes 30 minutes but allow 45 to savour the view. It is ideally suited for an evening. Although small the waterfall is very pretty and in lovely surroundings.

START At the parking area at the end of the tarmac road in Pentre Du.

DIRECTIONS Follow the A5 towards Capel Curig from the junction with the B5106 in Betws-y-Coed for almost a mile to where a small group of houses is seen up to the left. TURN LEFT at the signed road junction, then IMMEDIATELY RIGHT up the steep narrow road for 150 yards to the small parking area on the left where the tarmac ends.

TURN LEFT along a clearly seen path at the far end of the parking area. This is followed close to the stream up to a viewing area. There is a low stone wall here. Cross the rustic bridge to the right and continue up to the waterfall. The path veers away from the stream and continues up to join a track at a prominent 'sharks fin' of rock. TURN RIGHT. Follow the track down to where there is a power line pole on the right. TURN RIGHT 20 yards past this on to a narrow but obvious path. Follow this to join a track. TURN RIGHT and follow it back down to the parking area.

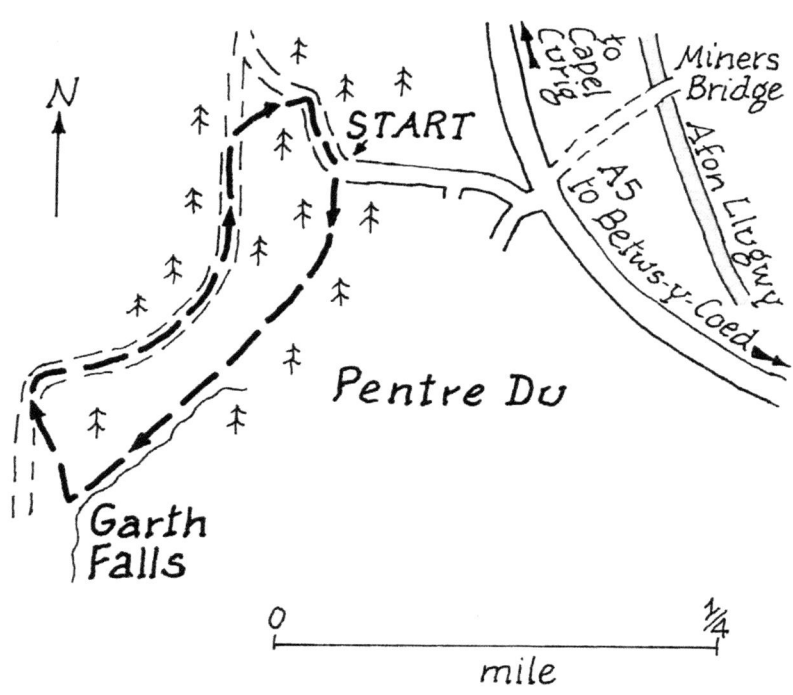

WALKS 4 & 5

WALK 5
LLANBERIS WATERFALLS

DESCRIPTION Although only 1½ miles this is a pleasant walk through woodland at the start before descending a steep road to reach the fine waterfalls by a delightful path. Allow 1 hour.

START Snowdon Mountain Railway terminus in Llanberis.

DIRECTIONS From any of the fee paying car parks nearby walk to the terminus.

1 Walk up the path by the side of the main road to a roundabout. Cross the minor road and continue ahead on the wide grass verge to a gate, finger post and ladder stile on the right. This is just beyond the Royal Victoria Hotel. Climb over the ladder stile and follow the path/track through Coed Victoria. Pass through a kissing gate and continue on the path gradually up and then along through a gap in the fence. Continue and pass through another kissing gate. The path passes between a wall on the left and a fence on the right to reach a gate by the Pen y Ceunant tea rooms.

2 Go through the gate to the very narrow minor road and TURN RIGHT down the steep road. Pass through the gate to the right of the cattle grid and continue to a road junction at a black finger post. TURN LEFT as indicated on the finger post to the waterfall. Continue along the road and pass under the viaduct of the Snowdon Mountain Railway. Ignore the right turning to Dol Elidir Blaen Ddol and continue along the road that bears left. TURN LEFT 50 yards further on at the sign for the waterfall.

3 Go through the kissing gate and walk up the road with a fence on the left. TURN LEFT again when the fence bears left and follow the path on the right of this. There is no sign here and the path easy to miss. Follow the path, passing under the railway viaduct again, to reach the Afon Arddu. Continue on the path on the right of the river passing some small waterfalls to reach the fine main waterfall. Retrace steps to the black finger post beyond which is a row of terraced houses, Vaynol Terrace 1906. TURN LEFT and continue down the road to the main road. TURN LEFT back to the start and your car.

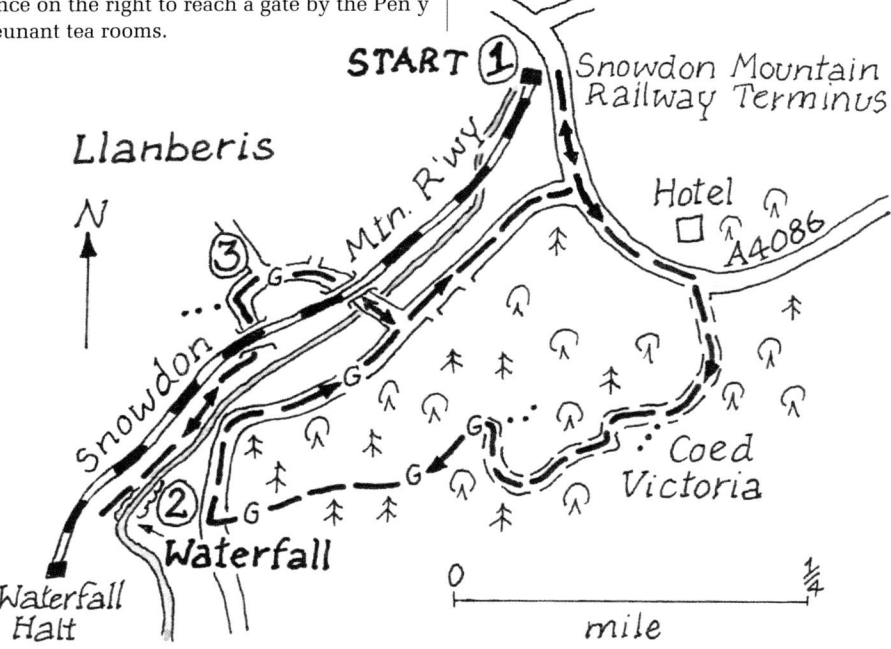

WALK 6
RHAEADR OGWEN, CWM CNEIFION FALLS, DEVILS KITCHEN & THE DEVIL'S APPENDIX

DESCRIPTION Rhaeadr Ogwen is a fine sight especially after heavy rain as it tumbles down in ever steepening drops. Although very close to the A5 it not often visited but is well worth the effort. Although only a very short excursion of ¼ mile it could be used as a precursor to walking around Llyn Ogwen or before the walk to view the mountain waterfalls. Even so 30 minutes can easily be taken to find the best vantage point. BEWARE of vertical drops.
The main walk into Cwm Idwal is a grand mountain experience best appreciated immediately after heavy rain when both Cwm Cneifion Falls and the Devil's Appendix will be in full flow. The Devil's Kitchen always has water flowing but again thunders through the rocky defile in wet weather. In dry weather the Appendix is a black streak down the cliff. However, when it does flow it is the highest single drop waterfall in Wales at 305 feet. In winter it forms a remarkable pillar of ice and is one of Wales' finest ice climbs. Allow 2 hours for the 2¾ miles walk.

START FOR BOTH WALKS From the Snowdonia National Park car park near to Ogwen Cottage where there are toilets and a snack kiosk.

DIRECTIONS From Betws y Coed drive along the A5 towards Bangor. Drive through Capel Curig and continue on the A5 below Tryfan to reach the sign at the far end of Llyn Ogwen indicating the car park. TURN LEFT into it. There is also a sign for the Youth Hostel. A small fee is payable but there are toilets, an information service and a snack bar here.

*R**haeadr Ogwen* can be appreciated in its own right without doing the main walk. From the car park return to the A5 and walk down the road away from the lake to the second gate on the left. Go through this and walk down disjointed and faint paths to admire the wonderful waterfalls. Return to the car park to start, if desired, the main walk.

1 From the car park cross the road to the snack kiosk. To the left of the Snowdonia National Park information office a constructed stone path leads off uphill. Continue to an ornate metal gate. Walk through this and cross a footbridge. Keep walking on this good path to reach a junction. BEAR RIGHT here on the wider path (left on the lesser path leads towards Tryfan) and continue to reach Llyn Idwal.

2 Go round the lake on the left and continue to a metal gate. Pass through this and continue almost to the foot of Idwal Slabs – *nicknamed 'Bumbly Hill' by rock climbers*. Continue walking uphill below Idwal Slabs on a well maintained path, but taking care at an awkward stream crossing, towards the Devil's Kitchen. Where the path enters a boulder field directly below the dark and brooding Kitchen it goes left uphill more steeply. However, down to the right, a small, but obvious path passes below a slabby boulder to the left. Pick your way down small rock steps to join a much more pronounced path. Follow this down, steep at first, to join with the path coming from the grassy sward.

3 Continue down to reach the lake shore just before a gate. Go through the gate and walk ahead for 100 yards to a path junction. BEAR LEFT here uphill on a narrow path. Cross over a path coming up from the right and continue easily to join a more pronounced path. TURN RIGHT along thios to reach a stile. Cross this and continue to the right of a rocky hump. *There are great views of the Nant Ffrancon to the left and ahead to Llyn Ogwen*. Descend to a fence and stile. Go over this and follow the path down to enter a narrow, rocky defile. Walk through this and down to a ladder stile. Cross this and con-

WALK 6

tinue to the main path. TURN LEFT to return to the car park.

Cwm Idwal is Wales' first National Nature Reserve and is perhaps the most dramatic. It is a perfect example of a landscape sculpted by glacial action. Rare arctic/alpine plants grow here such as three types of saxifrage, the purple, mossy and starry. Others include moss campion, Snowdon lily and globe flower. Sheep grazing has been removed from the whole of the area to encourage the regeneration of heather and other plants.

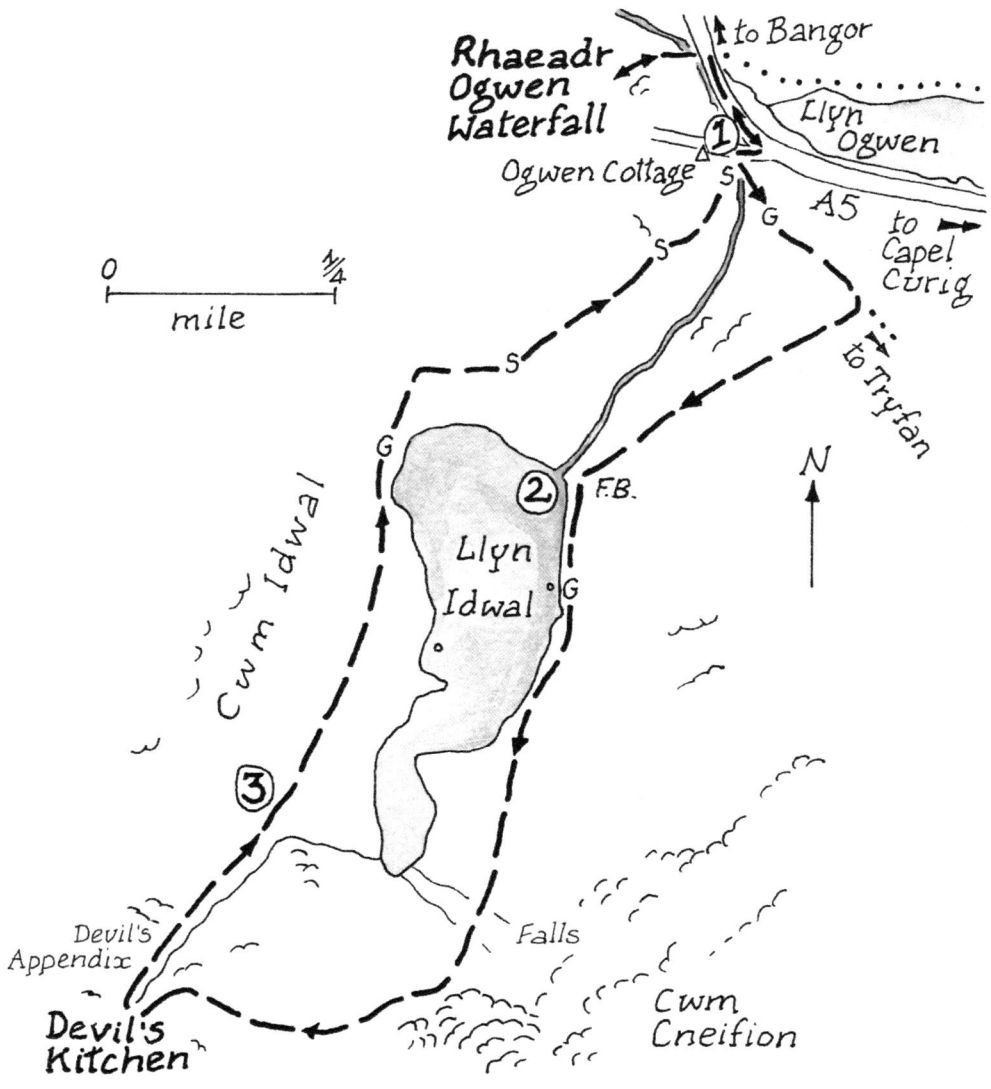

WALK 7
SWALLOW FALLS

DESCRIPTION Whichever way you decide to go round, the return walk will be uphill! This lovely 2½ mile walk visits one of the most popular and very scenic waterfalls in Wales, Swallow Falls, without having to pay for the privilege. Allow 1½ hours although it is easy to take longer.

START At the Ty'n Llwyn car park.

DIRECTIONS From Betws-y-Coed follow the A5 towards Capel Curig. At Ty Hydd (the Ugly House) TURN RIGHT and drive carefully up the very narrow minor road. The signed car park is ¾ mile along this on the RIGHT where there are some good views of the surrounding area. There are tables here for a pre or after walk picnic.

1 Walk past the picnic tables to the first of the yellow path marker posts. Follow the path into the wood and go past a large sign. Walk STRAIGHT ahead down the wide path passing marker posts at frequent intervals to join a wide track – BEWARE of mountain bike riders here. Walk diagonally across to a marker post and continue down to a track close to a 'Y' junction. GO LEFT and down the RIGHT HAND side of the 'Y'. The track goes down almost reaching the Afon Llugwy. Keep on the track to where it becomes a path. Follow this along with a fence to the right to a fenced descent to a fine balcony, complete with seat, and a fine view of Swallow Falls.

2 Return to the path and TURN RIGHT. Continue with the fence on the right and re-join the path. Follow it and descend to another viewpoint of the falls at marker post 20. Rejoin the path and TURN RIGHT. Follow the fence on the right along the very fine high level path with dramatic views down into the gorge below. When the fence ends GO LEFT as indicated along a track. GO LEFT again at a track junction and continue up to another track junction. TURN RIGHT along the track and continue to a marker post on the right opposite a flight of steps. TURN LEFT up these and follow a marked path through a cleared area of conifers. TURN RIGHT then LEFT and up slightly to reach a viewpoint. *This gives magnificent views of Moel Siabod 2,861 feet and Snowdon 3,560 feet from the rocky summit.* CARE is needed here as there is a rather long, vertical drop at this point. Return to the path and TURN LEFT. Continue up to the large sign seen on the outward walk. TURN RIGHT to go back to the car park.

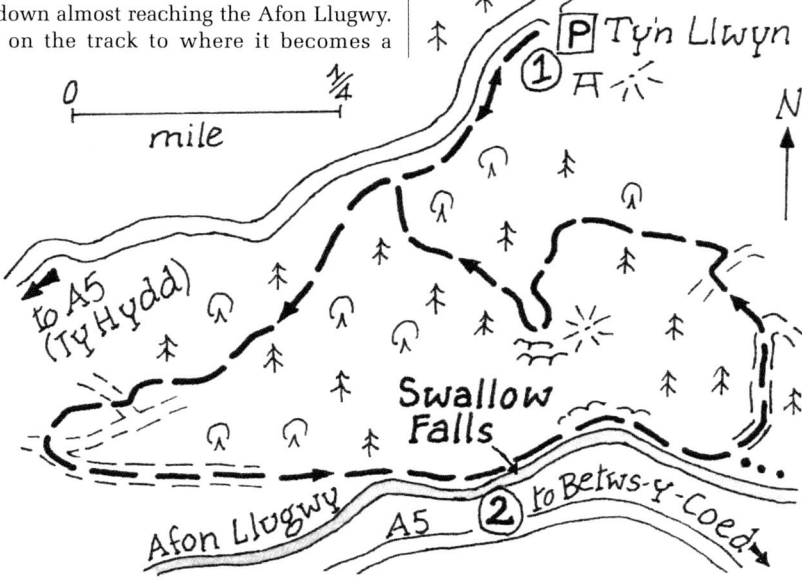

WALKS 7 & 8

WALK 8
CONWY FALLS

DESCRIPTION This is a spectacular and easy half mile walk taking around 30 minutes but allow 45 to savour the views of some fine and dramatic river scenery. A fee of £1 is payable (as at June 2013). There is a wonderful display of bluebells in the woodland here during spring.
START At the car park for Conwy Falls Café.
DIRECTIONS From Betws-y-Coed follow the A5 towards Llangollen. Drive past the right turning to Dolwyddelan and continue past the Silver Fountain Inn on the left. TURN RIGHT at the sign for Penmachno on to the B4406. The falls are also indicated, as is Ty Mawr. The large parking area is immediately on the RIGHT after turning.

The fine café building was designed by Sir Clough Williams-Ellis, the architect of Portmeirion, in 1957.

Having paid the fee pass through the many-barred turnstile on the right hand side of the café. TURN LEFT up the gravel path 10 yards ahead. Follow the path to reach a fence. With this on the left walk past several viewing points to where steps descend to the main one overlooking the very fine falls on the Afon Conwy, which are spectacular, especially after heavy rain. From the slate seat walk up very slightly and BEAR LEFT to follow the level path to where the end of a wall is reached. GO UP RIGHT here following the path back to the car park.

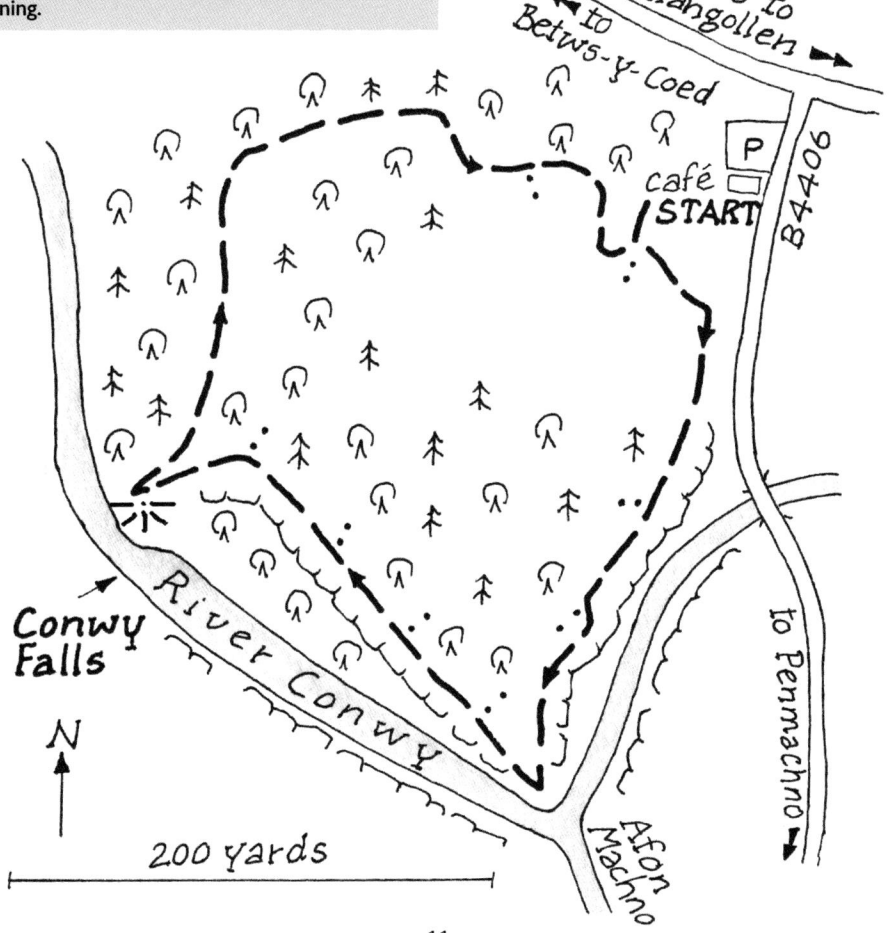

WALK 9
CYFYNG FALLS

DESCRIPTION This is a good 4½ mile walk. Cyfyng Falls are seen from the road just after starting the walk. These are very impressive during and immediately after heavy rainfall. Other smaller waterfalls are seen midway and towards the end of the walk. Views of the Snowdon massif are iconic and are best seen from close to Plas y Brenin.

START From the car park at Bryn Glo on the A5 in Capel Curig.

DIRECTIONS Follow the A5 from Betws y Coed towards Capel Curig. On entering the village the car park is clearly signed on the right. There is also a good café here for refreshment pre or post walk.

1 From the car park cross the road. TURN RIGHT and walk up the footpath, admiring the fine Cyfyng Falls on the Afon Llugwy below on the left, to Pont Cyfyng. TURN LEFT over the bridge and immediately RIGHT after crossing. There is a finger post here. Go through the gate and at the 'Y' junction immediately beyond TURN RIGHT, marker post. Follow the track down and cross a footbridge. Walk across the field passing to the right of a ruin to reach the Afon Llugwy. Continue upstream on the side of the river and climb over a ladder stile to enter the wood. At a path junction keep right still following the river to reach a metal footbridge.

2 Just before this TURN LEFT and go up following the path away from the river to a finger post. Continue AHEAD and then BEAR RIGHT at a 'Y' junction 10 yards ahead. The path goes up gradually to reach the end of a fence. Keep this to the right and follow the path above the river. The path levels off and in spring there is a fantastic display of bluebells along the next part of the walk. Pass to the side of a barrier and join a track. TURN LEFT along it and then RIGHT at a 'T' junction 60 yards further on. Continue along the track. At the junction with a track going right to Bryn Engan Farmhouse continue AHEAD through a gate. Follow the track and through another gate to reach Llynnau Mymbyr. Cross the footbridge on the right over the outflow of the lakes and through a gate. Follow the path up on the left hand side of Plas y Brenin and climb steps to a gate. Go through this to join the A4086.

3 TURN LEFT for 120 yards, cross the road to the right and over a ladder stile immediately before the de-restriction sign. Follow the track and continue straight ahead at a four ways junction. Keep following the track and through two gates 100 yards apart. The track continues to an isolated house on the right, Gelli. BEAR RIGHT just beyond this and go over a ladder stile. Follow the narrow tarmac road down through a gate to the right of a cattle grid into Capel Curig. There are toilets here and it is possible to break the walk to have a tea break in the café. Just up from the café and in the grounds of the Glan Dwr Mountain Lodge is a series of small waterfalls.

WALK 9

4 Cross the road from the café to the Celtic cross. Either, climb over the ladder stile or go through the gate and follow the track up and through a gap in the wall. Where the track goes left immediately beyond BEAR RIGHT on a path and follow it to a ladder stile. Climb over this to enter a wood. The path continues to reach three ladder stiles. Climb over the left hand one or go through the gate. Continue ahead with the fence to the right and again keep walking ahead when the fence disappears to reach a fine rustic bridge. TURN RIGHT, acutely, just before this and follow a tiny stream down on a feint path at first. The path very quickly becomes paved and continues alongside a fence on the left. Cross a fine clapper bridge and continue down past Bryn Tyrch Uchaf, a house on the left. Follow the path to the right of the fence and climb over a ladder stile or go through the gate to reach a track. TURN RIGHT down this and pass through a gate to reach a finger post and kissing gate. Go through this and BEAR LEFT to join the A5.

5 TURN LEFT and follow the footpath at the side of the road down to Cobdens Hotel. Cross straight across the road to the metal footbridge, seen on the outward walk, and cross over the Afon Llugwy. *There are some small waterfalls upstream of the bridge.* Go through the gate at the far side and scramble LEFT over rocks. Return to Bryn Glo from here by the outward walk.

Cyfyng Falls

WALK 10

PANDY & MACHNO FALLS INCLUDING FAIRY GLEN

DESCRIPTION This is a lovely 3¾ mile walk. Although much of the walk follows quiet roads and tracks it is nonetheless very scenic. The path towards the end of the walk follows a gentle line high above the Afon Conwy through fine woodland. A visit to the spectacular Fairy Glen is well worth paying the access charge. Currently this is 50p. Allow 2¼ hours.
START At the car park for Conwy Falls Café.
DIRECTIONS From Betws-y-Coed follow the A5 towards Llangollen. Drive past the right turning to Dolwyddelan and continue past the Silver Fountain Inn on the left. TURN RIGHT at the sign for Penmachno on the B4406. The falls are also indicated as is Ty Mawr. The large parking area is immediately on the right after turning.

The fine café building was designed by Sir Clough Williams-Ellis, the architect of Portmeirion, in 1957.

1 GO RIGHT out of the car park and follow the B4406 for ½ mile to the cross roads. TURN RIGHT and follow the very quiet road. *On the left just before the bridge over the Afon Machno is the old Penmachno woollen mill. Pandy Fall is seen to the left from the bridge whilst looking downstream will be seen the Roman Bridge.* Continue down the road ignoring a turning to the left to reach a group of houses. Opposite the garage of the last house, Pandy Mill, TURN RIGHT down the un-signed narrow path. This quickly reaches the fine Machno Fall. CARE is needed as there is an unguarded, long drop into river. Return to the road and TURN RIGHT. Follow it down with good views of Clogwyn y Gigfran, Giant's Head, ahead. BEAR RIGHT at the road junction and continue down to the A470 at the bridge spanning the Afon Lledr.

2 Cross over and TURN RIGHT. Follow the footpath to where it ends at Beaver Bridge. Carefully cross the road and the bridge. TURN RIGHT immediately beyond onto the track signed to Fairy Glen and Cwmanog Isaf Farm. Follow this to the entrance to Fairy Glen. TURN RIGHT through the covered gate where a 50p per person charge is levied. Follow the gravel path to the left and then BEAR RIGHT past a squat chimney. The path descends slightly to a path junction. Go STRAIGHT ahead, signed Riverside Walk. At the river bank BEAR LEFT and follow it to a 'Y' junction. Go up to the LEFT and continue rising above the river to a seat by a multi armed finger post. Continue AHEAD following the direction indicated to Fairy Glen. More seats are passed to reach a steep, often very slippery descent down steps to a huge boulder at the river's edge downstream of the breathtaking Fairy Glen, a narrow deep gorge. To return retrace your steps to the multi-armed finger post. TURN RIGHT, signed exit. Follow the fenced path to the next junction and TURN RIGHT following the path back to the track.

3 TURN RIGHT and through the small gate just ahead. Keep following the track and through the next gate. After going through a metal gate the track becomes a path. *This is delightful as it is high above the Afon Conwy river gorge.* Continue up the gently rising path, through another gate, until 15 metres before reaching the busy A5. Turn right down a few steps on a permissive path, part of the 'Slate Trail'. Continue below the fine embanked wall of the road to a flight of steps leading up into the car park and the end of the walk.

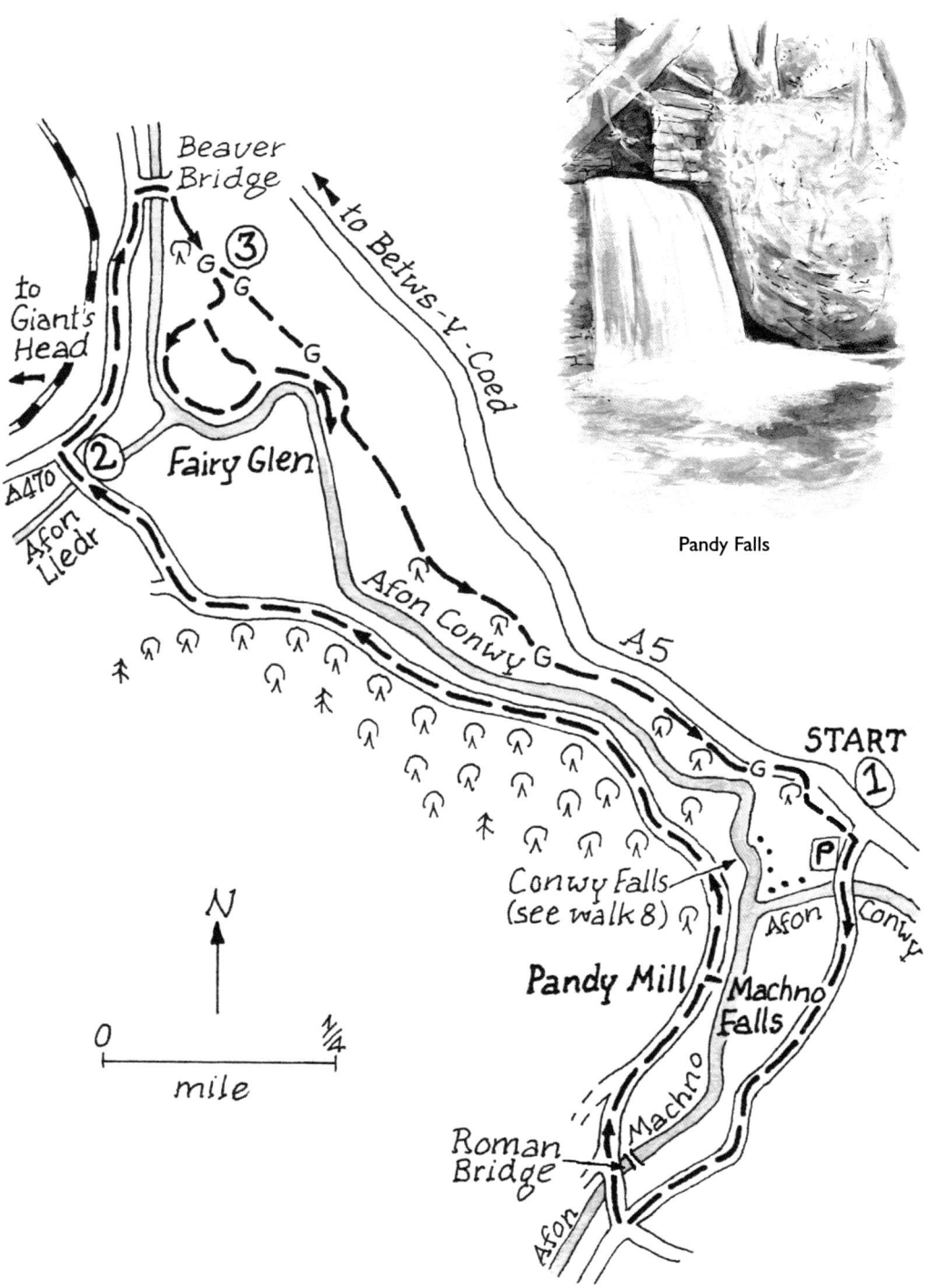

WALK 11
FRWD FERIN
(RHAEADR MYHERIN)
& NANT CHWARELMELYN WATERFALLS

DESCRIPTION This is a very adventurous 3 mile walk taking 3½ hours! Whilst half of the walk is on a track the other half is pathless. Towards the end, to reach the view of the stupendous waterfall, it is boggy and with much tussock grass. There is also a huge drop down into the deep ravine. This must be one of the most dramatic, remote and wild places in Mid Wales. It is well worth the effort to reach the viewpoint.

START By the side of the access road close to the turning down to Fagwr Fawr farm.

DIRECTIONS From Aberystwyth follow the A44 towards Llangurig. Drive past Nant yr Arian and through Ponterwyd. TURN RIGHT 500 yards past the B4343 turning to Devils Bridge. A finger post is directly opposite the turning. Continue along the rough lane to park off the road on the verge close to the turning down to Fagwr Fawr farm.

1 Walk to the turning down to Fagwr Farm, a finger post opposite this indicates the path. TURN LEFT down the track and follow it over a cattle grid and bridge to enter the farmyard. Go through a gate and walk to the right of the farmhouse. Follow the track up to and through another gate 50 yards further on. The track rises steeply and ends at a stile. This is where the almost pathless terrain begins. Cross the waymarked stile and continue slightly right following the line of the sedge filled hollow. A faint path develops and becomes a grassy track which disappears. Cross a peaty hollow and BEAR RIGHT diagonally on an intermittently feint path to reach a more pronounced one. This also disappears before reaching a col overlooking the largest of the Llyndoedd Ieuan lakes. BEAR RIGHT and descend to the outflow of the lake.

2 Cross this and BEAR RIGHT diagonally up a short rise. There are now no paths of any description! Walk in a south easterly direction to reach a fence and locate the stile in this. It is 20 yards before the fence corner. Cross the stile and contour around to the stream. Cross this, the outflow from the lake. *(Over to the left in the distance the*

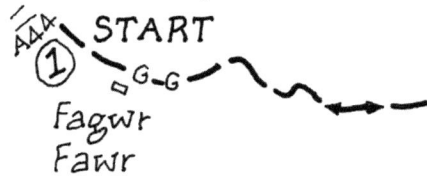

Nant Chwarelmelyn waterfall is seen at the base of a very deep ravine). The next ¼ mile is very time consuming, being littered with collapsing tussocks and bog between. Keep contouring, as much as possible over this very difficult and awkward ground, to reach a solitary and weathered marker post. TURN LEFT as indicated to the edge of the forest and find a way into it. A short descent bearing LEFT reaches the rim of the awesome, deep ravine, CARE. *From here there is an unrivalled view of the tremendous waterfall. No doubt you will have cursed and sworn crossing this ground but the effort is more than amply rewarded.* Return the same way back to Fagwyr Fawr

WALKS 11 & 12

WALK 12
AFON CROESOR WATERFALLS

DESCRIPTION This is a surprisingly fine 1½ mile walk. Although only taking 1½ hours it is quite feasible to spend much longer on hot summer days for swimming in the various pools or picnicking. Views of Cnicht and the Moelwyns as well of Snowdon are superb.

START At the lay-by at the far side of the bridge below Garreg Hylldrem.

DIRECTIONS From Porthmadog follow the A487 towards Penrhyndeudraeth. Turn left in the centre of the village on to the A4085. Continue through Garreg to a sharp left hand bend and along a 500 yards straight section of road towards a large looming cliff, Garregelldrem. Cross the Afon Croesor and park immediately on the left just beyond Pont Garreg Hylldrem in a large lay-by below the cliff.

1 Return to the bridge and cross over the road to a finger post waymark sign attached to the chevron marker. Pass through the gate to the right of the cattle grid and follow the track as indicated towards Felin Parc. Continue up the track on the left to pass above Felin Parc. *The Afon Croesor is seen tumbling below on the right.* When the track bears right follow the path STRAIGHT AHEAD, waymark. At the end of the cottage on the right is a marker post. Ignore the direction indicated. Instead continue SLIGHTLY RIGHT on a path to join the Afon Croesor. As the distinct path rises there are many small cascades and larger waterfalls up to 45 feet high. *In parts there is a very fine display of bluebells in spring.* This idyllic path ends at a wall.

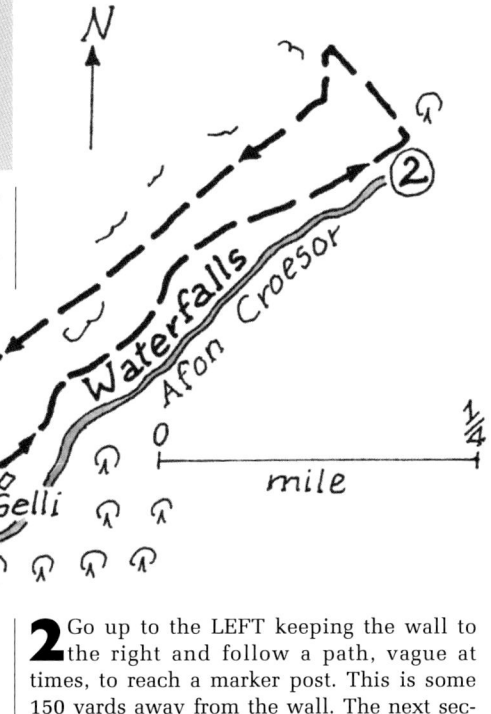

2 Go up to the LEFT keeping the wall to the right and follow a path, vague at times, to reach a marker post. This is some 150 yards away from the wall. The next section has some superb views. Continue down the broad ridge past a marker post and go through a gap in the wall. BEAR LEFT to a marker post. Descend the quite steep path through oak woodland to the marker post by the end of the cottage. TURN RIGHT to return to the lay-by.

WALK 13
AFON CWM LLAN

DESCRIPTION This is a very fine 4¼ mile walk in dramatic surroundings with terrific mountain vistas of Yr Aran (2,451 feet), Snowdon (3,560 feet) and Lliwedd (2,930 feet). Along with the fine waterfall there are many pretty cataracts. There is mining history thrown in for good measure. Although it is possible to continue up Snowdon on the Watkin Path this walk is very satisfying in its own right. Not to be missed. Allow 3 hours.

START At the Snowdonia National Park car park at Pont Bethania.

DIRECTIONS Follow the A498 from either the Capel Curig or Beddgelert directions to the car park for the start of the Watkin Path up Snowdon. The car park is on the left just before Pont Bethania if travelling from Capel Curig or on the right when coming from Beddgelert. There is a fee payable and there are toilets.

1 Cross the road from the car park and TURN LEFT. At the junction with a narrow minor road 100 yards further TURN RIGHT. Climb the steps ahead where a stone indicates the Watkin Path and go through a gate. Follow the pleasant path through the wood and across two footbridges. Pass through a gate just beyond these. Continue past an information board on the right and go through a gate to join a wide path. TURN LEFT up this and pass through another gate 25 yards further. Continue along the wide path. On reaching a bend to the left the falls first comes into view. Keep following the path with views of the fall to a gate.

2 Go through this and climb very gradually. There are many small cataracts in the Afon Cwm Llan below on the right. Just before the path levels there is a path junction opposite a weir. TURN LEFT and go up the old Braich-yr-Oen incline, *with superb views of Snowdon (3560 feet), Yr Aran (2451 feet) and Lliwedd (2946 feet)*, to reach a level tramway. TURN LEFT and follow the tramway to where it ends at the top of the Hafod y Llan incline for superb views. DO NOT DESCEND THIS. Retrace steps and keep following the tramway all the way to where it becomes lost in a marshy section. Cross this and pass in front of the ruined Hafod y Llan slate mill. BEAR RIGHT across a bridge spanning the stream and go slightly up to pass behind the ruined barracks to the Watkin Path.

3 TURN RIGHT down this and continue past a fine slab of rock on the left to reach the small rocky hump of Gladstone Rock on the right. The path continues down passing the ruined Plas Cwmllan and crosses a footbridge. Continue down past the point where the outward walk turned off to reach the gate passed on the outward walk. Continue down to the car park.

On 13th September 1892 William Ewart Gladstone the Prime Minister of Britain for the fourth time delivered a speech from what became known as Gladstone Rock, to 2,000 people to open the Watkin Path. This was named in honour of Sir Edward Watkin a Liberal Member of Parliament and railway entrepreneur. He had retired to a chalet in Cwm Llan. In order for visitors to be able to walk up Snowdon Sir Edward created a path from the already existing one up to the slate quarries to the summit of the mountain. It was the first designated footpath in Britain and the first step towards the opening up of the mountains and countryside for walkers. Gladstone was 83 at the time of his speech!

There are the remains of several copper mines dotted around Cwm Llan one of which was Braich yr Oen. The incline of this mine meets the level slate quarry tramway. This continues to the Hafod y Llan slate quarry which operated from 1840 to around 1880. The now ruined Plas Cwmllan was once the slate quarry manager's house. This was used by commandos during their train-

WALK 13

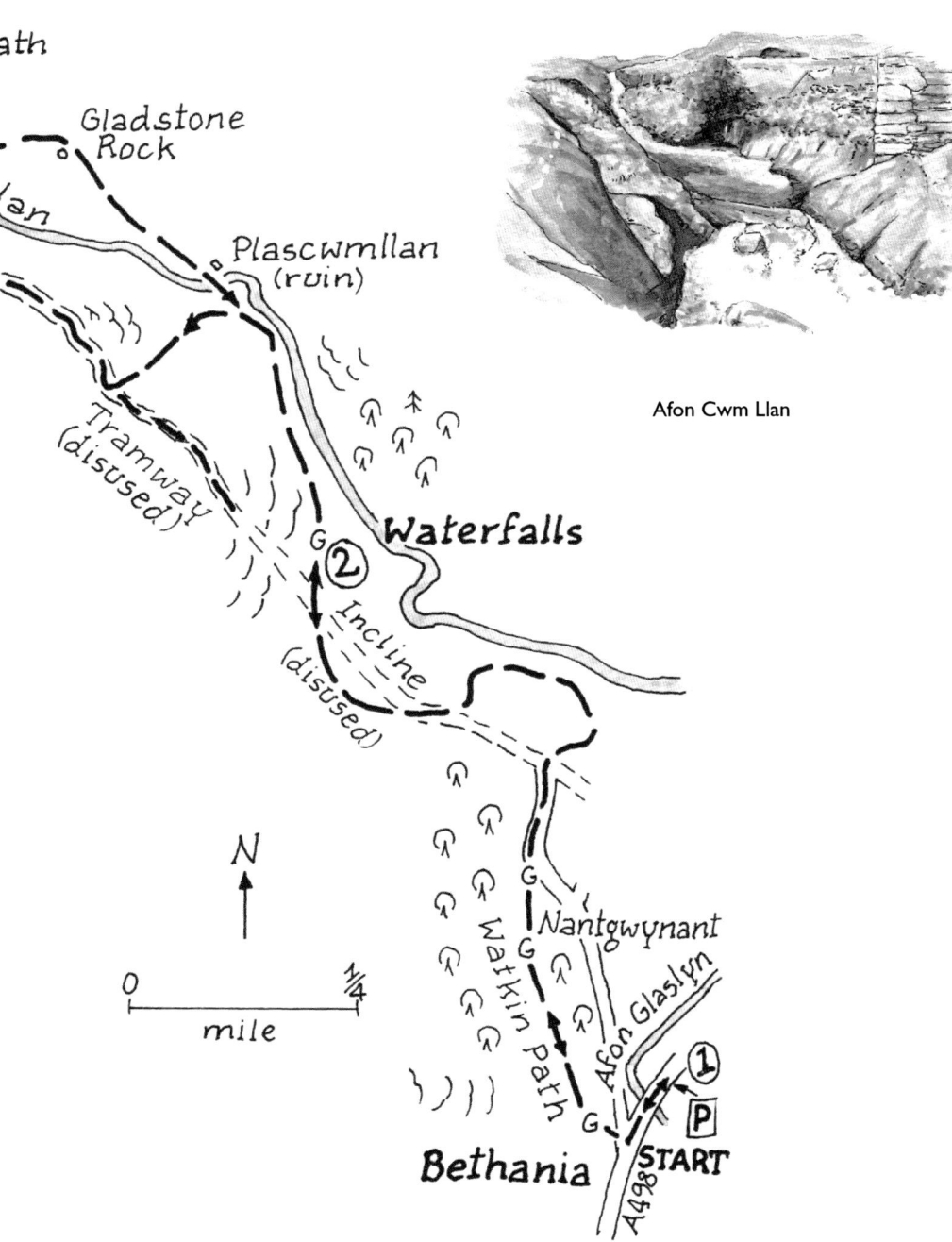

Afon Cwm Llan

ing in the Second World War. Bullet holes are visible in the walls.

WALK 14
NANTCOL WATERFALLS

DESCRIPTION Although short this is a very pleasant 1½ mile walk. There are superb views of Moelfre, Rhinog Fach and the highest point in the range, Y Llethr. There are some fine cataracts as well as a dramatic but small waterfall. Allow an hour.

START At the large car park at the Nantcol caravan and camp site.

DIRECTIONS Follow the A496 from either the Barmouth or Harlech directions into Llanbedr. Turn off this road by the Victoria Inn where there are signs for Cwm Bychan, Cwm Nantcol and Rhaeadr Nantcol. Drive up the road through Pentre Gwynfryn and turn right over the bridge spanning the confluence of the Afon Artro and Afon Cwmnantcol. Signs also indicate Cwm Nantcol and the waterfalls. TURN LEFT 100 yards further, again following the signs to Cwm Nantcol and the waterfalls. Drive up the steep hill and continue to where signs indicate the Cwm Nantcol campsite. Turn right here and descend into the car park where a fee is charged. NOTE. The car park is only open *between 10.00 and 18.00.*

1 From the car park go through the gate by the reception office/camp shop. TURN LEFT and follow the track to a 'Y' junction. BEAR RIGHT and follow the track to where it ends in a wide grassy track from which a wide path continues close to the river. Climb over the ladder stile. *There are some pretty cascades to the right and a great view of the main waterfall from here.* Continue up a flight of steps to the top where the path splits. There are way markers and many danger signs!

2 Follow the right hand path. Spaced, blue topped marker posts are now followed. The path descends to a marker post close to the river. BEAR LEFT and continue past several small but pretty cascades. Fine views develop as height is gained. *Out to the coast, Moelfre (1,913 feet) the dominant hill to the right whilst Rhinog Fach (2,336 feet) the left hand of the two skyline peaks and Y Llethr (2480 feet) are seen ahead.* Cross straight over a small meadow and BEAR RIGHT then slightly LEFT. Continue to reach the edge of an obvious marshy area. The path now goes up to the LEFT and continues to reach the edge of a wood.

3 Walk down this, keeping the fence to the right, to reach a ladder stile. Climb over this to where the trees are more dense. Follow the path down to reach a wall. TURN LEFT and keeping the wall to the right continue to a ladder stile. Climb over this and bear slightly LEFT. Continue easily and along to a ladder stile down to the right. TURN RIGHT and climb over this into the camp site and car park.

WALK 15
HENGWM WATERFALL

DESCRIPTION A mighty waterfall in a quiet valley is visited after walking along a track and struggling through brash. The struggle is well worth the effort however. The valley is very quiet. A pleasant walk back ensues once the tracks have been left behind. Allow 1¼ hours for the 1½ mile walk. *Note that the stream will be impassable in very wet weather.*

START At the left-hand side of the wide forest road 100 yards beyond the end of the tarmac.

DIRECTIONS From Machynlleth follow the A489 briefly towards Newtown. Just beyond the tyre and exhaust garage TURN RIGHT onto the mountain road signed to Forge, Dylife, Aberhosan, Llyn Clywedog and Llanidloes. TURN RIGHT in Forge, before crossing the bridge, signed for Uwch y Garreg. Ignoring all turnings continue to where a steep descent leads to the end of the tarmac. The parking area is on the left 100 yards further on.

1 Walk along the forest road to a junction. TURN UP TO THE RIGHT and follow the rising track to reach a cross roads and TURN RIGHT. The deteriorating track descends to a stream where there is a pile of logs. Cross the stream carefully. BEAR LEFT and up to a partially concealed, brash-covered rough track. After 150 yards head over to the left to a fine vantage point for the fall. Return to the cross roads.

2 Cross STRAIGHT over the main forest road and follow the rising track to another track junction. TURN LEFT and go through a gate 25 yards ahead. Follow the grassy track pleasantly down to cross a footbridge. BEAR LEFT through a gate and continue straight ahead at the junction with the track coming down from the right. The track crosses a concrete bridge over the Afon Hengwm to reach another track junction. BEAR RIGHT back to the parking area.

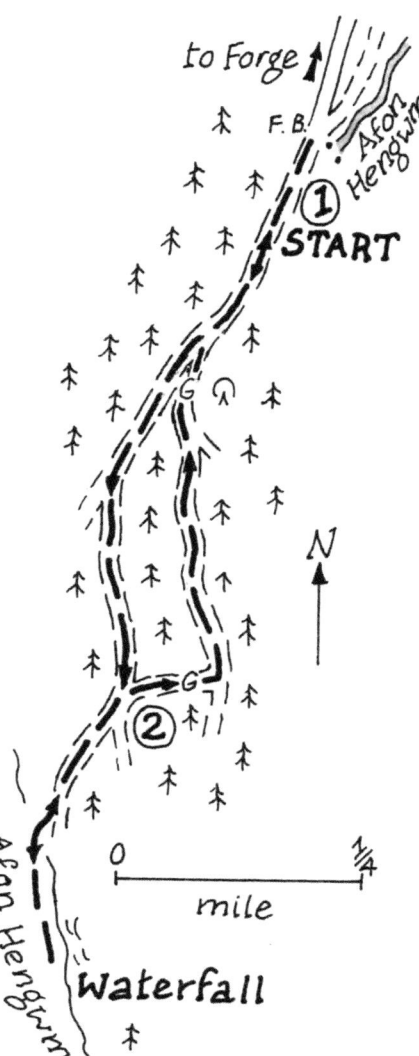

WALK 16
RHAEADR CWM DYLI

DESCRIPTION A pleasant 3½ mile walk in beautiful surroundings. Although the views of the waterfall are not very close they show their impressive nature. Allow 1¾ hours.

START At the Snowdonia National Park roadside car parking area near to the Pen y Gwryd.

DIRECTIONS Follow the A4086 from the Capel Curig direction to the Pen y Gwryd. Go past this and the right turn for Llanberis. Continue to the car parking areas to the left or right of the A498 just beyond the turning. Or from the Beddgelert direction follow the A498 to the car parking areas. There is a fee payable.

1 From your car walk towards a prominent finger post indicating the way to either Nantgwynant or Pen-y-pass. TURN RIGHT through the kissing gate and cross a footbridge. Follow the constructed path up and then slightly down to reach a finger post. TURN LEFT very sharply and follow the path down to reach the valley floor. Cross the footbridge over the stream on the right, small cataract above.

2 Continue down to the left and cross under the power line by the power line pole. Keep going down with the power line to the right. *The pointed peak above the pipe line is Gallt y Wenallt (2,031 feet).* The path wanders around to the left of the power line here. There are some short sections of marshy ground. Keep to the right of the substantial wall. *As Cwm Dyli Power Station is approached the lower Cwm Dyli waterfall comes into view up to the right.* Just before the path enters a small group of conifers the middle and higher falls come into view. Continue keeping the wall and then fence to the right and go through a gate to join a track.

3 TURN LEFT up this and through the fine metal gates (if closed it will be necessary to ford the river 150 yards upstream). Continue up the track for 250 yards and turn up to the left on the less pronounced track. Follow this to reach the main track. *There are good views of the waterfall, with Crib Goch 3,028 feet towering behind, from here.* TURN LEFT and follow the track, with views of the summit triangle of Snowdon 3,560 feet far above, back to the car parking area.

Cwm Dyli hydro-electric power station was built in 1905 by the Porthmadog, Beddgelert and South Snowdon Railway Company. The scheme was backed by the North Wales Power and Traction Co Ltd to supply electricity to its own electric railway and connected slate quarries and mines. The railway was planned to run through the valley but ran short of funds and, thankfully for the area, the attempt was abandoned. Electricity produced here was also used to power the Long Wave Wireless Telegraph transmitting station built near Waunfawr by Marconi in 1912.

It is Britain's oldest power station and is one of the world's original grid-connected hydro-electric stations. It still supplies power directly to the National Grid. First commissioned in 1906 it has supplied power almost continuously, apart from being closed for upgrading in 1990. A single turbine now produces up to 9.8 megawatts.

It is known locally as the 'chapel in the valley' because of its exterior design. It once employed thirteen men but is now controlled remotely from Dolgarrog in the Conwy valley.

Water for the site primarily comes from Llyn Llydaw, some 1050 feet above and is carried from the lake through a one-and-a-quarter mile long pipeline, This featured in the James Bond film 'The World Is Not Enough'.

WALK 16

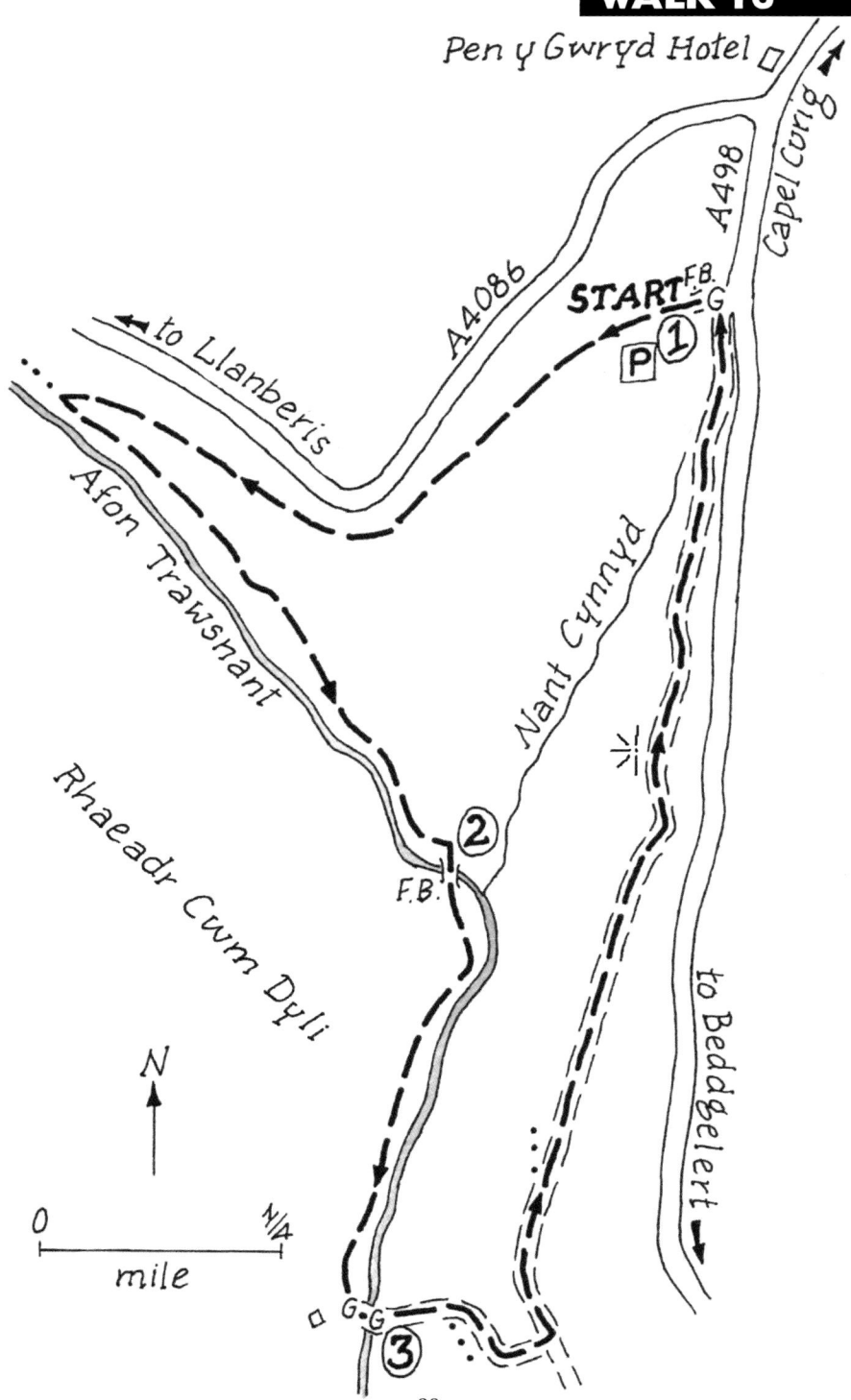

WALK 17
MAESGWM WATERFALL

DESCRIPTION This waterfall is situated in a very quiet and secluded valley above Dolwyddelan. The 2½ mile walk is along roads or tracks with a short section of path. Although the walk does not approach the fall there are good views of it from many places. Allow 1¼ hours.

START At the parking area close to Tai Penamnen.

DIRECTIONS From Betws-y-Coed follow the A5 towards Llangollen. Cross the Waterloo Bridge and TURN RIGHT on to the A470. This is followed to the village of Dolwyddelan. TURN LEFT opposite Y Gwydyr Hotel. There is also a Spar shop on the corner. If coming from the south TURN RIGHT off the A470 opposite Y Gwydyr. Continue along this road and over two bridges, one over the railway and the other the river. TURN RIGHT immediately after the second bridge on the road signed to Benar Terrace. Follow this road ignoring all turnings to where it develops a grassy strip in the middle. Continue to the ruined village of Tai Penamnen. There is a signed parking and picnic area 150 yards ahead on the left. A finger post indicates the path to Pont Carreg Alltrem.

1 Continue up the road along the valley to where the tarmac ends. There is a house on the left. Continue along the gravel track and go through a gate, way marker, passing in front of the holiday cottages. *Looking up to the right from here Maesgwm waterfall is easily seen.* Pass through another gate at the far side of the cottages. Follow the track over two small bridges and BEAR LEFT at the 'Y' junction, finger post. The track shrinks to a path after the second bridge. Follow it up through conifers to a track.

2 TURN LEFT along this with good distant views of the waterfall. The track rises then descends very gradually to reach a finger post on the left indicating Pont Carreg Alltrem. *The vertical cliff above the track is Carreg Alltrem, a favoured haunt of rock climbers.* TURN LEFT and cross the bridge to reach the car park.

The first house at Tai Penamnen was built in the 15thC, possibly during the War of the Roses. It was a one roomed cottage that had an inglenook fireplace utilising a lateral chimney. In the 16th century Maredudd ab Ieuan the founder of the Wynn's of Gwydir, built an extension to each side to the cottage. Not only did it protect against the weather but also against lawless brigands terrorising the area during that time. At the start of the 18th century Angharad James rented the house and the whole valley from the Wynn family. She was an attractive woman well known for her knowledge of the legal system. She was also a poet and musician. When Angharad was twenty she married William Pritchard, 40 years her senior. As an accomplished harpist she played at a place dubbed clwt y ddawns (dancing place) whilst her maidens danced. In the 19thC two more houses were built creating quite a thriving little community with over 30 people living there. However, by the beginning of the 20thC only one family remained and shortly after the First World War the village was abandoned completely.

WALK 17

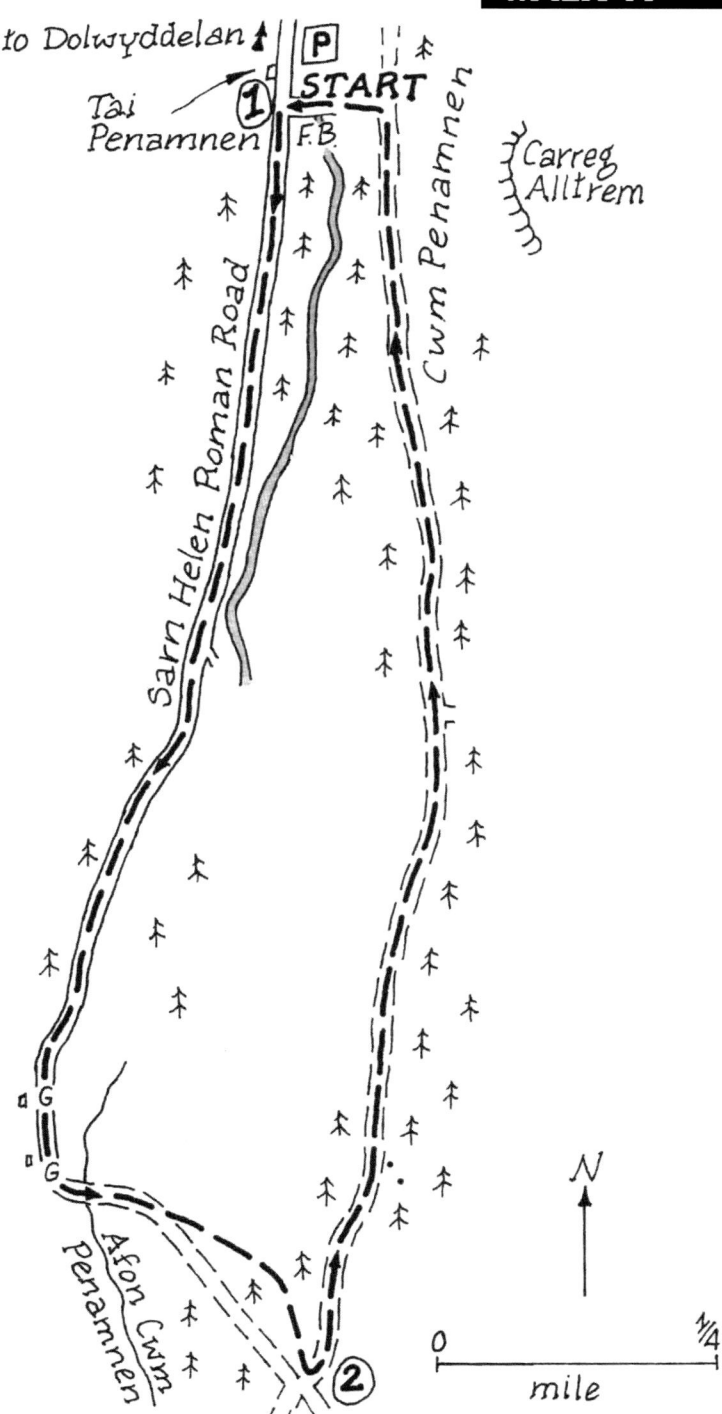

WALK 18
PISTYLL GWYN

DESCRIPTION One of several waterfalls in Wales bearing the same name this is a pretty 3½ mile walk beneath the dramatic and barren Rhinoggau. Allow 2¼ hours. Although much of the walk is on forest tracks the section in the trees is on paths that are not often travelled. The area is quiet and has an air of solitude about it.

START At the end of the tarmac road in the pull in beyond the gate on the minor road leading to Graigddu Isaf.

DIRECTIONS From Dolgellau follow the A470 towards Betws y Coed. Continue through Ganllwyd and past the right turn towards the Coed y Brenin Visitor Centre. Check your odometer here and drive for another 2 miles to an unsigned turning to the left. This is 600 yards past the phone box in a lay-by on the right hand side of the road. TURN LEFT here and almost immediately drive through a gate. The narrow road continues for another 2 miles to another gate. Go through this. Immediately beyond is a signed parking area.

1 From the parking area follow the right hand track. (The signed track straight ahead becomes very boggy!). Follow the track ignoring the right hand turning to reach the farm. Pass through the gate at the end of the farm and continue along the track to where it bends to the left. TURN RIGHT where signs indicating the Roman Steps and a waterfall are seen. Follow the good path to reach some steps. *At the top of these the waterfall is close by on the right.* Climb a further series of steps and continue to join a track. There are marker posts here.

2 TURN RIGHT and follow the undulating track to reach some ruins on the right. Three hundred yards past these are two marker posts, one each side of the track. The right hand one is ten yards beyond the left hand one and there is a large lay-by to the left just beyond. TURN RIGHT at the right hand marker and follow the faint path down with a wall to the right at the start. Marker posts help to identify the way but the path becomes more defined. Cross a footbridge and continue through the forest past more marker posts to meet a forest track. TURN RIGHT and follow it down to where it ends. A marker post is seen to the left. Cross the stream to reach a small but pretty lake.

3 Keep to the left and cross a small footbridge. At a marker post drop down to the stream and follow the path along the edge of it to where the path veers to the right at a low wall. Keeping the wall to the right follow the path down to reach a junction with a track, marker post. Cross STRAIGHT over and follow the path again with marker posts guiding the way to reach a ladder stile. Climb over this and walk towards the farm. Climb over a stile to the left of long low house and cross the farmyard to reach the track of the outward walk. TURN LEFT up this back to the car parking area.

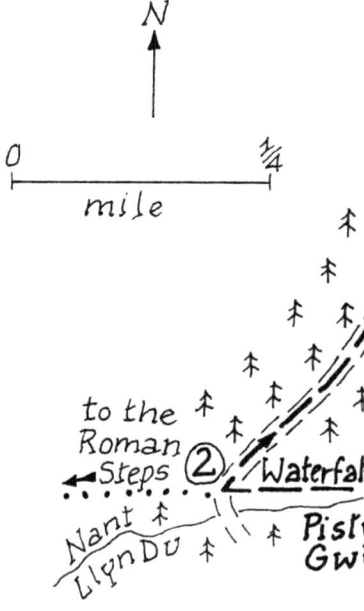

WALK 18

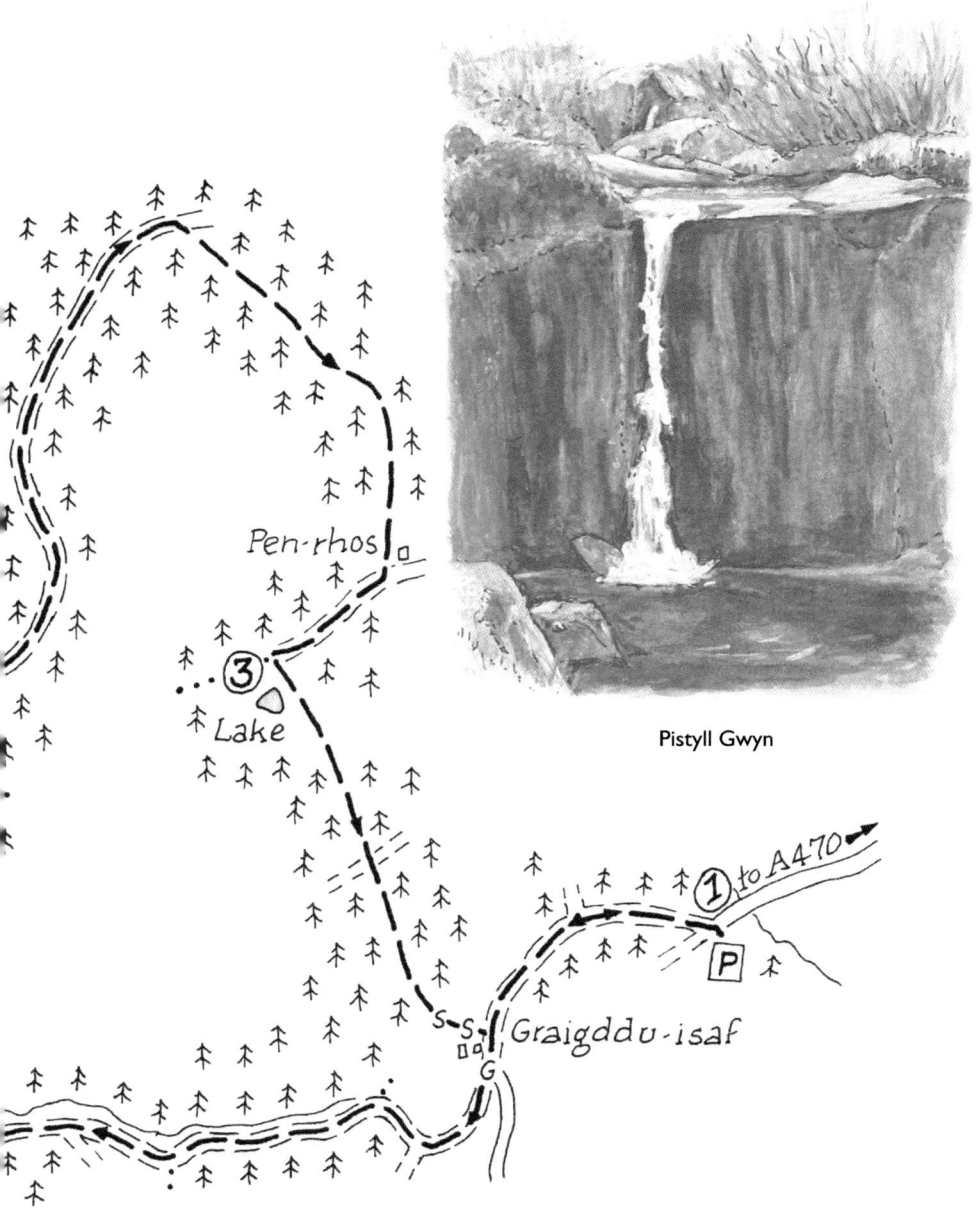

Pistyll Gwyn

WALK 19
RHAEADR CYMERAU

DESCRIPTION This is a lovely and quite easy 1¼ mile walk. There is some very pretty woodland, a dramatic river gorge with a fine series of beautiful waterfalls. Allow an hour for the walk but expect to take longer in this wonderful place. The walk is clearly marked by way markers.
START At the large looping lay-by by the side of the A496. This is 200 metres before the turning to Manod.
DIRECTIONS From Blaenau Ffestiniog follow the A496 towards Porthmadog. Drive past turnings to Tanygrisiau and continue down the hill and past the turning to Manod. Turn right 200 yards past this into the large looping lay-by. This is the third lay-by when coming from Blaenau Ffestiniog. When coming from the Maentwrog direction follow the A487 and turn left on to the A496 towards Blaenau Ffestiniog. Turn left at the junction with the B4391 still following the main road. The car park is the first of three lay-bys.

From the car park go through the kissing gate and follow the track. There is an information on the left. Continue until just before reaching a garage. The main track continues straight ahead. TURN RIGHT and down to go through the gate. Follow the rougher track down to the fine footbridge over the Afon Goedol. Cross this. TURN RIGHT immediately after crossing over and walk up by the side of the fence to view the beautiful series of lower falls. Return to the bridge. Cross this once again and walk back up the rough track to a gate on the apex of the 90 degrees left hand bend.

Pass through this and follow the path to the garage mentioned above by the side of the main track. TURN RIGHT. Continue along the track to a gate, marker post. Go through this. Follow the track up to where a gate ahead leads into the farm. DO NOT go through this.

Instead go through the kissing gate on the LEFT. Bear slightly right and pass through another kissing gate 80 metres further. Walk to the right of the out building on the wide path and through the kissing gate 100 metres further. Walk past a seat. *There are great views of Manod Bach 1,676 feet and Manod Mawr 2,169 feet from here.* Pleasant walking continues to a path junction with a marker post. BEAR LEFT ignoring the stile on the right and go through another kissing gate. *There is grand view of the Moelwyns here with, left to right, Moelwyn Bach 2,329 feet, Craigysgafn 2,260 feet and Moelwyn Mawr 2,526 feet.* The obvious and easily followed path continues past another two seats to arrive at the track of the outward walk. TURN RIGHT back to the lay-by.

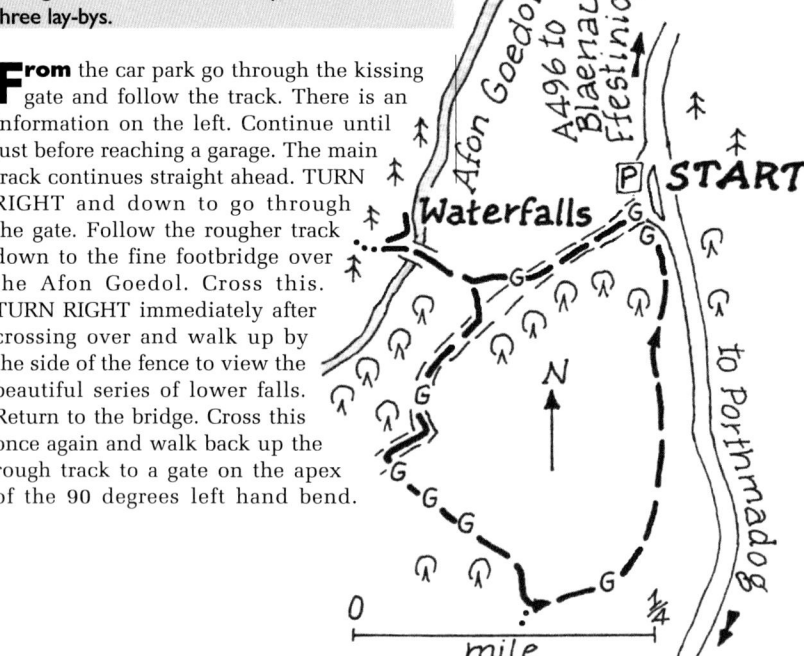

WALK 20
PISTYLL RHAEADR

DESCRIPTION This iconic waterfall on the Afon Disgynfa, becoming the Afon Rhaeadr after the waterfall, is often quoted as the highest in Wales. In fact, although it is a mighty fall, it is only ninth for single drop waterfalls and 17th for tallest total height. The walk around to the top is quite fine and other smaller, but pretty, feeder waterfalls can be seen. DO NOT get too close to the edge. This is abrupt and it is a long way down! There are some good views down the valley.

START At the large lay-by just before the end of the tarmac road.

DIRECTIONS From Bala follow the B4391 through Rhos-y-gwaliau to the junction with the B4396 at Pen-y-bont-fawr. Take this road to the junction with the B4580 and TURN LEFT to Llanrhaeadr-ym-Mochnant. Pass the Wynnstay Arms pub in the village and then TURN RIGHT into Waterfall Street. A sign indicates the way to the waterfall. After 3½ miles of narrow road there are some large lay-bys on the left for parking. There is another car park 200 yards further on for which a modest fee is charged.

1 Walk up the road to the fee paying car park and café. From here take the signed riverside path to reach a footbridge spanning the river flowing from the base of the waterfall. At the near end of the footbridge a finger post indicates the way to the top of the waterfall. Take this path. After a short rise the path levels and passes through a gate to join the main path. Follow this and go through a kissing gate at the edge of the wood.

2 TURN LEFT 10 yards ahead where another finger post shows the way forward. This path is steep but it zigzags making the going easier and reaches a track. TURN LEFT up this to where it levels. Down to the left an information board can be seen close to a finger post by a kissing gate. TURN LEFT and descend to these and go through the kissing gate. Continue down quite steeply to the river. There are small but very pretty waterfalls tumbling down before the final plunge of the main fall. APPROACH WITH CARE. DO NOT try to cross to the other side.

3 Return to the track and TURN RIGHT. To avoid the steep descent of the path follow the track down all the way to the edge of the wood and then back to the lay-by.

*P*istyll Rhaeadr is one of the 'Seven Wonders' of Wales. The other six are – Wrexham Steeple, Snowdon's Summit (without the people!), Overton Yew Trees, Saint Winifred's Well, Llangollen Bridge and the Gresford Bells. The fall, as mentioned above, is not the highest in Wales, but is still 60 feet higher than Niagara Falls!

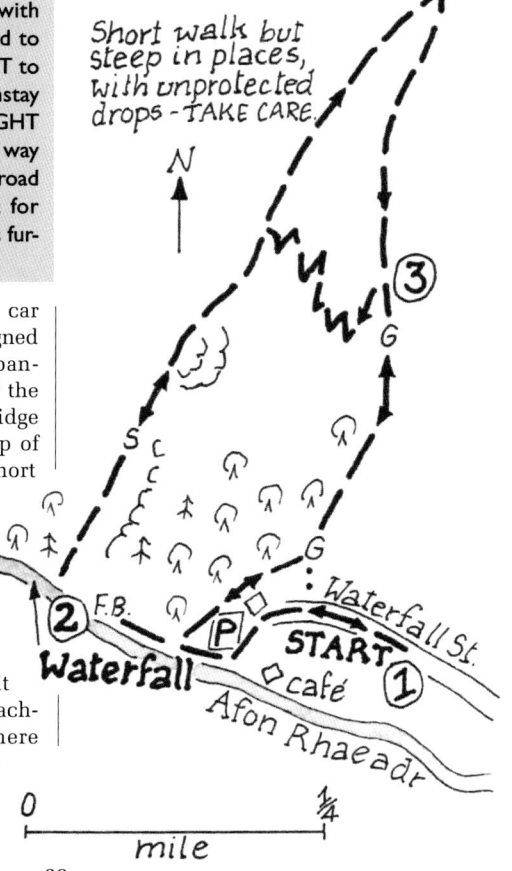

WALK 21
PISTYLL BLAEN-Y-CWM

DESCRIPTION This very grand waterfall on the Afon Tanat is reached at the head of a quiet and remote valley. It is very important to keep to the footpaths in this area. The scenery is splendid and there are two ways to appreciate this waterfall. One is from a high vantage point with superb views over the surrounding area and the other from below. Although each option is only 3 miles allow 2 hours for either of these walks.

START At the car park for Saint Melangell's church.

DIRECTIONS From Bala follow the B4391 through Rhos-y-gwaliau to Llangynog. TURN RIGHT in the village and follow the signed road to Pennant Melangell. This is a very narrow road. The car park is on the right next to the church. NOTE. There is no other parking further up the valley.

Walk up the road past the dead end sign until a gate with a waterfall sign is reached on the right. TURN RIGHT through this gate. There is a finger post indicating a bridleway. Go up the edge of the field with the fence on the right past a marker post to a gate. Go through this and walk diagonally LEFT to the next marker post. Continue in the same line to the next gate. Pass through this to reach a finger post. TURN LEFT and keeping the fence to the left continue for 100 yards to the fence corner and a four-way junction. A grassy track goes down to the left. Two options avail themselves here for seeing the waterfall:

OPTION 1 Cross straight over the track. Take the distinct grassy and highest path. Follow this across the hillside, gradually rising. As height is gained superb views open up and Pistyll Blaen-y-cwm is seen ahead plunging over 300 feet down from the moorland above. The path ends at a stream where it is prudent to turn back. DO NOT attempt a descent into the valley from here. It is extremely steep and adorned with waist high gorse bushes! Return the same way back to the car park.

OPTION 2 From the four-way junction cross over the track and take the less clear path below the high path. This is much narrower but level. It crosses the hillside to reach a fence on the left. Continue to where the fence ends and where the path has all but disappeared. Bear left and down to the stream. This is easily crossed in low water conditions. Continue up to the impressive waterfall. NOTE: Due to access restrictions it is important to return the same way because there is no access via Tyn-y-Cablyd.

Before or after the walk it is recommended that you visit the 800 years old church, the only one dedicated to Melangell. The yew trees in the churchyard are over 2,000 years old.

There is a legend associated with Melangell, derived from two 17thC transcripts of a lost medieval Life of Saints. A prince called Brochwel was out hunting one day in Pennant when his hounds raised a hare that took refuge in a thicket. On pursuit the prince found a virgin praying with the hare hiding under her skirt. The hounds were urged forward but fled howling. The huntsman raised his horn to his lips but was unable to remove it. The virgin told the prince that she lived at this place and that she had fled here for refuge. The prince was so impressed with her godliness that he granted the valley to her where she founded a religious community.

There are carvings of hares in the church along with the shrine to Saint Melangell.

WALK 21

Saint Melangell's Church

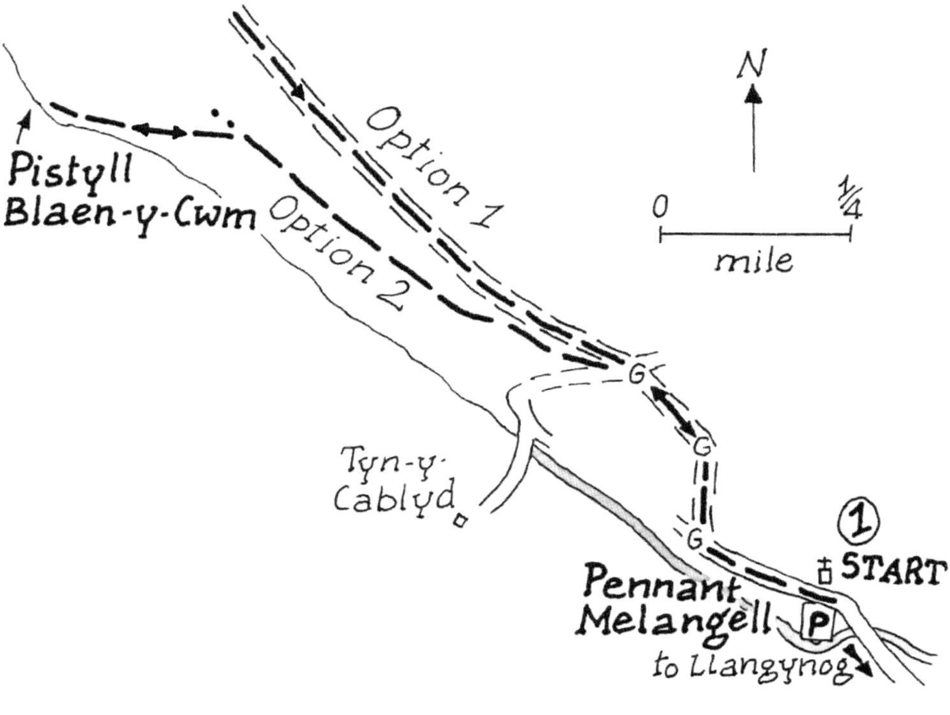

WALK 22
CWM DWFN FALLS

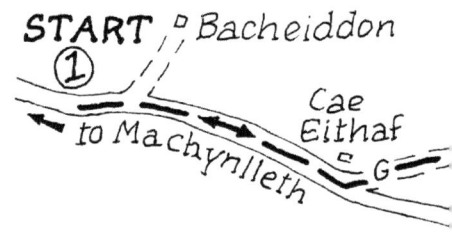

DESCRIPTION A very pleasant 4½ mile walk with only one short, steep section. The views are stunning. Farmland predominates with the walk following tracks for much of the way. Allow 2½ hours.

START At the lay-by in the small abandoned quarry on the left 100 yards before Bacheiddon.

DIRECTIONS From Machynlleth follow the A489 briefly towards Newtown. Just beyond the tyre and exhaust garage TURN RIGHT onto the mountain road signed to Forge, Dylife, Aberhosan, Llyn Clywedog and Llanidloes. Check your odometer here. Continue up this road ignoring all turnings to left and right for five miles to a lay-by, the remains of a small quarry, on the left of the road where cars can be parked. This is 100 yards before the access road to Bacheiddon.

1 Walk up the road past the access road for 500 yards to the unsigned Cae Eithaf farm on the left, a large bungalow set back from the road. There is often a green wheelie bin here for Rhoswydol. TURN LEFT along the track and through a gate after 100 yards. When the track splits 800 yards further follow the higher of the two. This is more or less level and continues past a recently excavated mine entrance and passes through a gate. There is now a fence to the left and the track continues to a barn. TURN LEFT immediately beyond the end of the barn through a gate. There is a white-topped gate post on the right. Descend the short steep slope to a decaying footbridge.

2 Cross this and go through the gate immediately beyond. TURN RIGHT through the gate 10 yards ahead. Walk up the steep field alongside a line of trees to reach the fence overlooking the Nant y Fedw ravine. Follow this fence up to a gate. DO NOT go through this but TURN RIGHT and follow the fence up and through the gate 10 yards to the right of the fence. Follow the track up to where it bends to the left. Before doing so walk ahead for 30 yards to view the very fine Cwm Dwfn waterfall. Return to the track and follow it up to where it disappears. Continue in the same line to reach a faint grassy path. Follow this to where it starts to rise. BEAR LEFT to reach a fence and a good but often muddy track. Follow this and cross a small stream to reach a large area of sheep pens. Keep on the track and pass through three gates through the pens. BEAR LEFT after the third gate following the defined track first slightly up then gradually down to reach a gate before the track rises again. Go through the gate and follow the track up to reach a track junction.

3 Take the LOWEST track down to the LEFT and follow it through a gate to reach another close to Rhoswydol. Pass through this and another 50 yards ahead to reach the access road to Rhoswydol. BEAR LEFT and follow the good track down and through a gate near the Afon Crewi. Go through the gate and carefully cross the river via large stepping stones. Follow the track up to the RIGHT past another recently opened mine entrance to the track junction of the outward walk. Continue AHEAD up the track to return to the mountain road. TURN RIGHT to the lay-by.

WALK 22

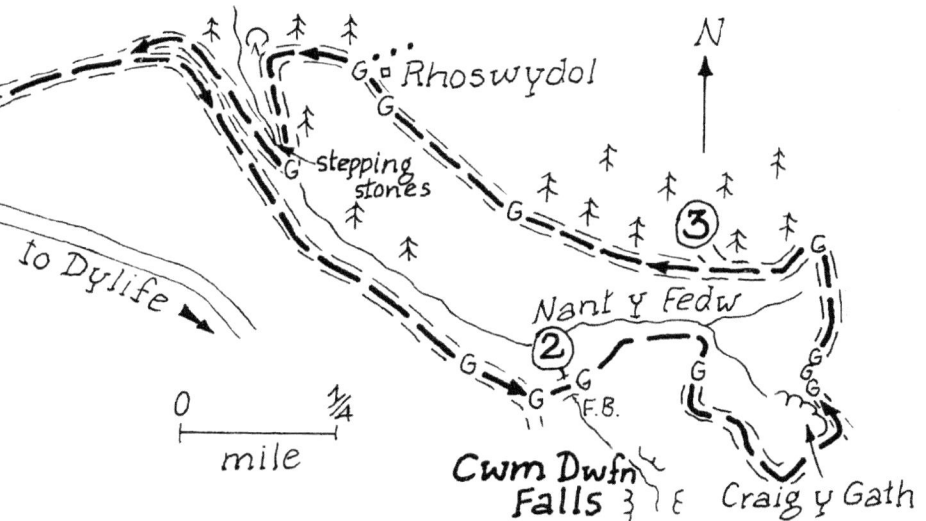

Cwm Dwfn Falls

WALK 23
DULAS GORGE FALLS

DESCRIPTION Although short this is a very pleasant 1¼ mile walk. The steep V sided gorge the falls tumble down is spectacular whilst the views from the summit of Moel Fadian are superb. Allow 1¼ hours.
START At the lay-by 25 yards beyond the track junction.
DIRECTIONS From Machynlleth follow the A489 briefly towards Newtown. Just beyond the tyre and exhaust garage TURN RIGHT onto the mountain road signed to Forge, Dylife, Aberhosan, Llyn Clywedog and Llanidloes. Continue until the summit is reached and a sign for the Nature Reserve is seen. TURN RIGHT here along the rough track. WARNING: cars with low clearance need to park before going down the track. If driving, continue down for 850 yards to where a track branches off to the right. There is a lay-by on the right 25 yards after the track junction to park cars.

1 A faint path leaves the lay-by and heads towards the obvious fence corner. The path VEERS RIGHT 100 yards before it. Continue 50 yards or so above and parallel to the fence then BEAR LEFT to it when the path disappears. Continue past the right angled fence corner to reach a 'V' shaped fence corner overlooking the dramatic, deep 'V' shaped gorge with the waterfalls plunging down the Afon Dulas in the base of the ravine. Return to the lay-by, or before doing so continue up Foel Fadian (1,850 feet) for superb views of the surrounding area.

2 The fence runs up the steep grassy hillside. Follow it up for 100 yards and then go diagonally right under the base of the grassy knoll to reach a track. TURN LEFT and follow it past a marker post on the left to another one on the left. There is a yellow topped post on the right here. TURN RIGHT and follow the faint path up and across the steepening hill towards the next yellow topped post. The path continues 200 yards to the left of the post to the summit of the hill. There are terrific views from here. Return to the track and follow this back to the lay-by.

WALK 24
RHAEADR WEN

DESCRIPTION This is a fine 3¾ mile walk with some lovely views. A dramatic view of the small waterfalls in the very steep ravine can be reached with care. The walking is mainly on tracks apart from the section around Glaslyn. Allow 2¼ hours.
START At the Glaslyn car parking area.
DIRECTIONS From Machynlleth follow the A489 briefly towards Newtown. Just beyond the tyre and exhaust garage TURN RIGHT onto the mountain road signed to Forge, Dylife, Aberhosan, Llyn Clywedog and Llanidloes. Continue until the summit is reached and a sign for the Nature Reserve is seen. TURN RIGHT here along the rough track. WARNING: cars with low clearance need to park before going down the track. Continue down the track past the track junction for walk 23, to reach a cattle grid. TURN RIGHT just before this to reach the Glaslyn car parking area.

1 Return to the track and TURN RIGHT over the cattle grid. Follow the track for 650 yards to a junction. Continue ahead ignoring the left hand track. Cross another cattle grid. There is a lovely view of Glaslyn and Foel Fadian here. *When the track levels there is a great view of Pumlumon.* Continue to cross another cattle grid, lovely view of the lake of Bugeilyn. Pass through a gate by the barn just before the ruins of the farmhouse Bugeilyn. Continue another 120 yards to a track junction.

2 Go up to the RIGHT and through a gate almost immediately. Follow the track to where there is another wonderful view of Bugeilyn and Llyn Cwm-byr. Continue to the dam. (It is possible to continue further from here by walking below the dam and crossing the substantial footbridge. Follow the track to reach a hollow with a tiny stream, Rhaeadr Ddu, flowing below the track. The

WALKS 23 & 24

waterfall of this stream very rarely flows and is best not visited as access is poor and not advised. If doing this add another mile and 30 minutes walking time). From the large lay-by above the dam bear left across tussock grass to reach the top of the Rhaeadr Wen stream. The ravine deepens quickly. Follow the edge of this with CARE to a tremendous vantage point atop a grassy knoll. Return to the dam.

3 Return along the track to where there is a sharp right hand bend on the level section and where a less pronounced track leaves the main one. TURN LEFT along this. At first it goes STRAIGHT ahead then BEARS RIGHT and continues to reach a fence. TURN RIGHT alongside this and follow it down to Glaslyn. TURN LEFT and follow the path through two gates 300 yards apart. Continue along the gravel shoreline path around the lake to a sign indicating the way to a viewpoint. TURN LEFT to this – *where there are fine views of the ravine below, Foel Fadian with its trig point on top, Cadair Idris and the Tarren range of mountains.* Return to the lake and TURN LEFT. Go through a gate and over a footbridge spanning a tiny stream. Continue to the car parking area.

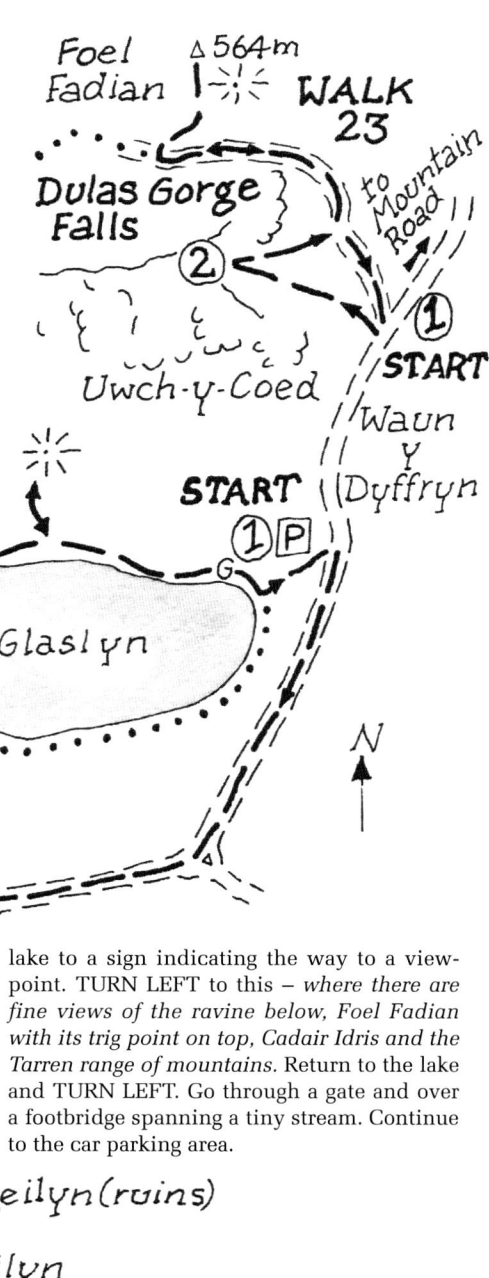

WALK 25
WATERFALLS ON THE AFON TARENNIG

DESCRIPTION This is a 5 mile mountain walk taking 2¾ hours. Although the waterfalls can be seen at a distance on the outward walk and can easily be visited directly from the start, the ascent of Pumlumon 2,467 feet is very worthwhile. The views from the summit are good and the waterfalls, although small, are attractive.

START At the car park on the A44 at Eisteddfa Gurig.

DIRECTIONS From Aberystwyth follow the A44 towards Llangurig. Drive past Nant yr Arian, through Ponterwyd and Dyffryn Castell. Continue around a sweeping horseshoe bend to reach the high point on the road. The car park is on the left - a fee is payable.

1 Walk up to the farm buildings and through these to a finger post on the right indicating a bridleway. TURN LEFT and walk up to and through a gate to the right of a cattle grid. Continue up the track after passing through two gates in quick succession to a 'Y' junction. BEAR LEFT and continue up to the edge of a wood where the track bends right. Continue alongside the wood and climb over a stile on the right hand side of the track. Continue following the track to where it levels and veers away from the wood. At a post on the left TURN LEFT on a faint path and follow the edge of the wood to go over a stile. BEAR RIGHT and continue up to a gate in a fence.

2 DO NOT go through this but TURN RIGHT. Keep the fence to the left and continue up to and over a stile and then BEAR RIGHT to reach a good path. Follow this up to climb over a stile to reach the summit.

3 Climb back over the stile and walk down on a bearing of 160 degrees to reach a faint path and a line of cairns. Follow these as the path becomes much clearer before it disappears. A line of weathered but spaced wood posts are followed bearing slightly left to reach a good track. TURN RIGHT down this and go over a stile. Continue for 250 yards and descend the grass slope carefully to view several small waterfalls in the Afon Tarennig. *Note how the stream has cut down to form the gorge.* Return to the track and continue following it down and through a gate at a junction of tracks. Continue ahead and through another gate to reach the track of the outward walk by the farm. Return to the car park.

Pumlumon, often anglicised to Plynlimon, is also known as 'The Five Peaks'. It possibly means something entirely different as it is virtually impossible to identify five peaks on this featureless ground. Plynlimon or Pumlumon derives from Roman origins – Plumbilimenis meaning lead boundary, which it is. Romans mined extensively hereabouts. Over time the Latin ending was dropped, like many others, and the name Plumlimen emerged. This explains the first 'l' and is a much truer spelling to that found on older maps. It seems a pity to drop the 'l' in an attempt to make it 'Pum', or five, as this obscures the Roman origin.

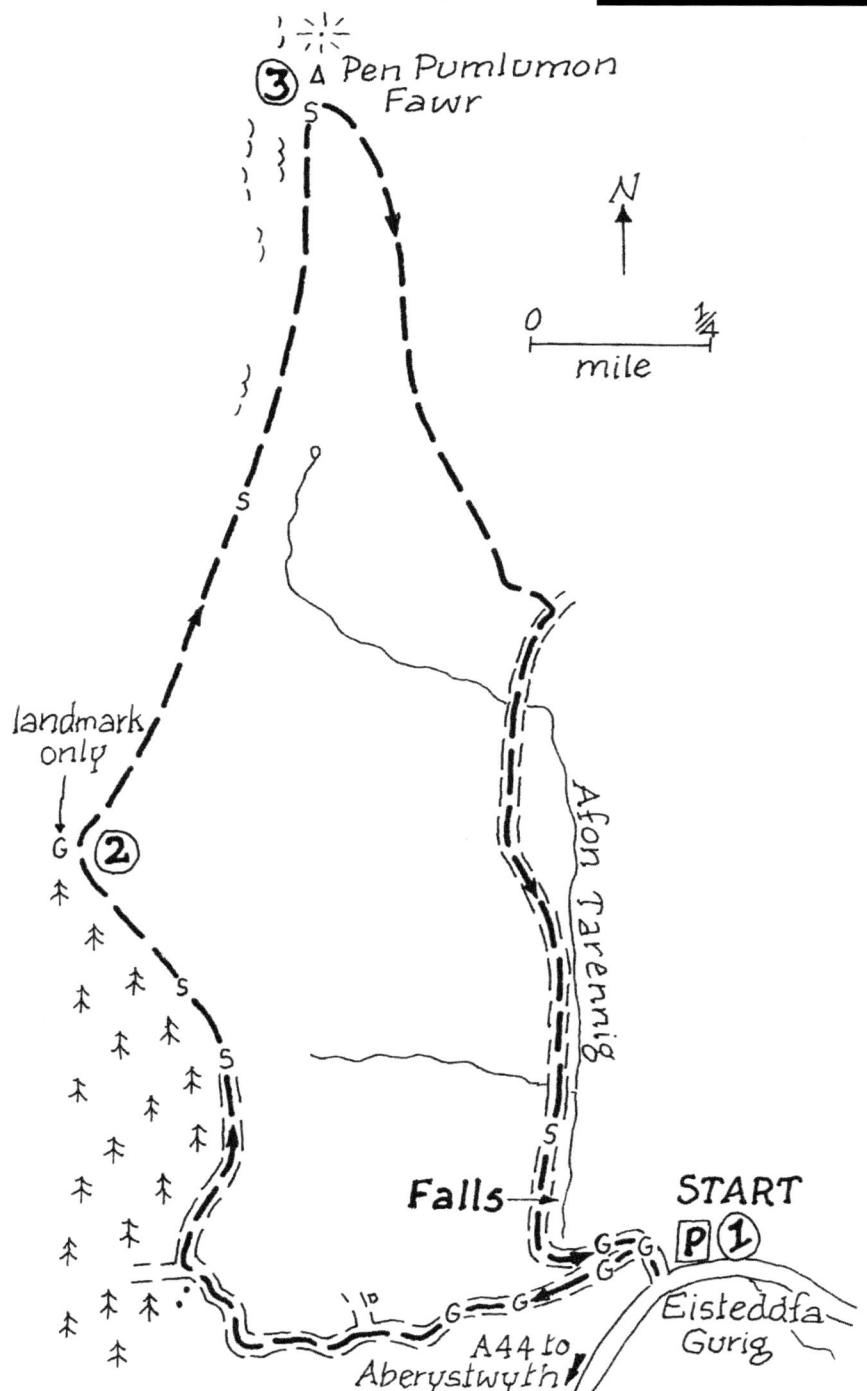

WALK 26
AMARCH FALL

DESCRIPTION This hard, challenging, but fine 4¼ mile walk is only recommended for experienced walkers used to traversing steep ground. Commencing down the B4405 and then the very quiet minor road alongside Tallyllyn the walk reaches the ruined Pentre Farm. Here it leaves the road to climb steeply up to the remote waterfall before continuing up a broad ridge with increasingly fine views to reach the Minffordd Path which is descended to the very dramatic Llyn Cau, snuggling below the frowning cliffs of Craig Cau. The final section of the walk descends to the right of the Cadair Cataracts and back to the car park. Allow 4 hours.

START At the car park at Minffordd as for the Minffordd path up Cadair Idris.

DIRECTIONS From Machynlleth follow the A487 towards Dolgellau. Drive through Corris to the road junction with the B4405, signed to Tywyn. TURN LEFT here and almost immediately RIGHT into the Minffordd car park. From Dolgellau follow the A470 towards Dinas Mawddwy as far as the Cross Foxes junction. TURN RIGHT on to the A487. Follow this to the B4405 turning for Tywyn. TURN RIGHT and almost immediately RIGHT into the car park. A fee is payable, but there are toilets.

1 From the car park walk past the toilet block to a kissing gate to the right of it. Go through this to join a track. Cross over this slightly left on to a wide gravel path. Follow this to reach another gate. Go through this and TURN LEFT 5 yards ahead down a narrow path to join the B4405 after passing through a metal kissing gate. TURN RIGHT down the road. Where the road turns sharply to the left there is a very narrow road going straight ahead. Go through the gate and follow this road to a ford. This is avoided by crossing the footbridge on the right. Carry on down the road passing through three gates.

2 After passing through the third gate TURN RIGHT up a farm track to go through the next gate, way marker. There is a long low barn on the left. Follow the track almost to the house. TURN RIGHT just before this to a way marker on a fence post. GO RIGHT through a wide gap in the fence and follow the path up and go over a ladder stile to the left of a gate. The path hugs the fence on the left and gives great views down into the stream gorge. *The stream has many fine cascades and cataracts.* When the fence crosses the stream CAREFULLY follow the right edge of the stream to reach an open area. Escape upwards and follow the line of the stream some 100 feet above it, picking out the easiest line as there are no visible paths! There is a very steep grassy slope descending into the stream. A narrow path is eventually reached and leads across to the stream again 100 feet below the main waterfall. There is a long wide boulder gully ascending on the far side of the stream at this point. Climb up a grassy rib on the right of the stream to the fine waterfall.

3 From here climb up a very steep grassy rib CAREFULLY on a narrow path to reach a much clearer one. TURN LEFT along this to the top of the main waterfall and continue up to the topmost falls below the wild and desolate Cwm Amarch, Go up and RIGHT from here for 100 yards and then ascend the grassy slope on the left bearing DIAGONALLY RIGHT. Head towards a rocky knoll seen below some quartz-speckled rock over to the left. The final steep section to the summit, crowned with some very fine quartz rock, is tackled on the front face. From the summit cross a short level section and then bear steeply up and DIAGONALLY RIGHT to suddenly reach a path. TURN RIGHT along this to join the Minffordd Path.

Cwm Amarch Falls ③

4 TURN RIGHT down this and descend to Llyn Cau nestling in the fine glaciated cwm. *In wet weather, or just after, there are many long streaks of white water descending the steep slopes of Cadair Idris.* The path descends much more easily to the Nant Cadair at a junction of paths. Continue down to reach this and go through a gate. A long series of steps descend close to the very fine Cadair Cataracts on the left. *There are a several viewpoints on the way for these.* At the

WALK 26

Minffordd Path to Craig Cwm Amarch & Cadair Idris Summit

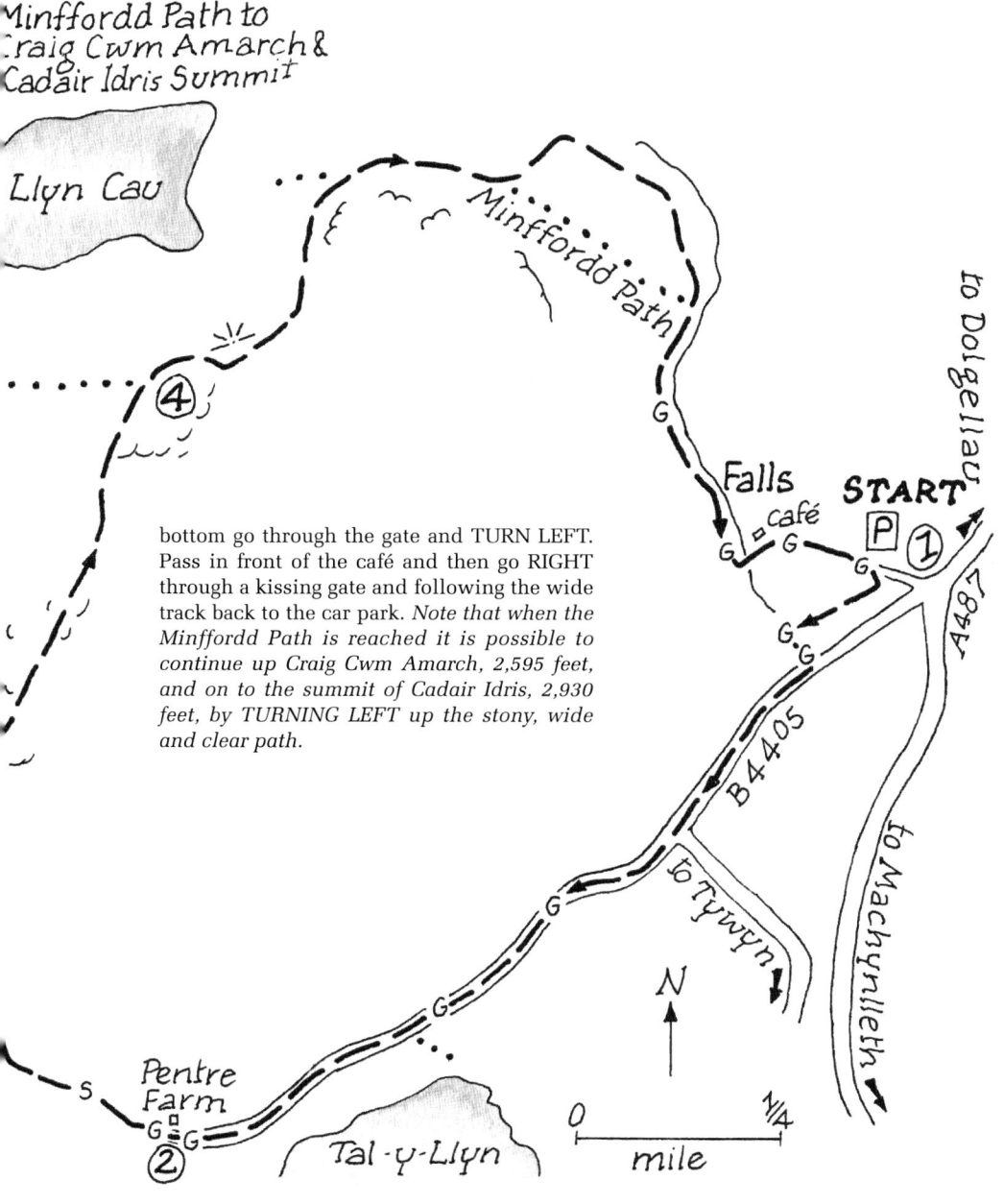

bottom go through the gate and TURN LEFT. Pass in front of the café and then go RIGHT through a kissing gate and following the wide track back to the car park. *Note that when the Minffordd Path is reached it is possible to continue up Craig Cwm Amarch, 2,595 feet, and on to the summit of Cadair Idris, 2,930 feet, by TURNING LEFT up the stony, wide and clear path.*

PRONUNCIATION

Welsh	English equivalent
c	always hard, as in **c**at
ch	as in the Scottish word lo**ch**
dd	as th in **t**hen
f	as f in o**f**
ff	as ff in o**ff**
g	always hard as in **g**ot
ll	no real equivalent. It is like 'th' in then, but with an 'L' sound added to it, giving 'thlan' for the pronunciation of the Welsh 'Llan'.

In Welsh the accent usually falls on the last-but-one syllable of a word.

KEY TO THE MAPS

- ⇢ Walk route and direction
- ═ Metalled road
- ─ ─ ─ Unsurfaced road
- • • • • Footpath/route adjoining walk route
- ～ River/stream
- 🌲 Trees
- ▬■▬ Railway
- **G** Gate
- **S** Stile
- F.B. Footbridge
- ☼ Viewpoint
- **P** Parking
- **T** Telephone

THE COUNTRYSIDE CODE

- Be safe – plan ahead and follow any signs
- Leave gates and property as you find them
- Protect plants and animals, and take your litter home
- Keep dogs under close control
- Consider other people

Open Access
Some routes cross areas of land where walkers have the legal right of access under The CRoW Act 2000 introduced in May 2005. Access can be subject to restrictions and closure for land management or safety reasons for up to 28 days a year. Details from www.naturalresourceswales.gov.uk
Please respect any notices.

About the author, Des Marshall

Des has had a lifelong interest in mountaineering, climbing, walking, canyoning and caving. As well as being an advisor, trainer and assessor in outdoor activities, he has undertaken many expeditions worldwide but now focuses more on local excursions. After moving away a couple of years ago, the lure of the plethora of exciting walking and climbing became too much and he now lives in Talysarn, near Caernarfon.

Published by **Kittiwake Books Limited**
3 Glantwymyn Village Workshops, Glantwymyn, Machynlleth, Montgomeryshire SY20 8LY
© Text & map research: Des Marshall 2018
© Maps & illustrations: Kittiwake Books Ltd 2017
Drawings by Morag Perrott
Cover photos: Main: Pistyll Rhaeadr, Llanrhaeadr-ym-Mochnant. David Perrott. *Inset:* Fairy Falls, Trefriw. Des Marshall.

Care has been taken to be accurate.
However neither the author nor the publisher can accept responsibility for any errors which may appear, or their consequences. If you are in any doubt about access, check before you proceed.
Minor revisions 2018.
Printed by Mixam, UK.

ISBN: **978 1 908748 29 4**